THIS is a summary of Mr. Gore[n]... od as presented in his book, PO[...] DING. It is bound into this book for your convenience. The publisher suggests that you tear this page at the perforation and put it into your pocket or bag for reference—so that any moot bidding situations can be settled at the bridge table with the utmost cordiality.

This summary is printed again at the end of the book, just in case you lose your pocket copy.

SIMON AND SCHUSTER, PUBLISHERS
Rockefeller Center, N. Y.

Raise partner's suit bid to 2 with 7 to 10 points
Raise partner's suit bid to 3 with 13 to 16 points
Make a jump shift with 19 points
Show a new suit at 1 level with 6 points
Show a new suit at 2 level with 10 points
With hands counting 11 or 12 points find two bids without forcing partner to game.

The Take-out Double

A take-out double should be based on a hand of the same strength as an opening bid, that is, 13 points for a double of a suit bid.

An immediate double of 1 No Trump therefore should be based on 16 points.

When partner responds in a suit for which you have good support, revalue your hand as dummy.

As responder to a take-out double: if you have 6 points you have a fair hand, 9 points a good hand, and 11 points a probable game.

As partner of the opening bidder, after a take-out double, pass with a poor hand, redouble with a good hand, and bid immediately with a moderate hand.

A SUMMARY OF THE GOREN POINT COUNT METHOD OF CONTRACT BIDDING

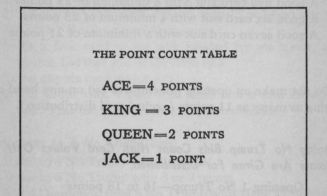

THE POINT COUNT TABLE

ACE = 4 POINTS

KING = 3 POINTS

QUEEN = 2 POINTS

JACK = 1 POINT

26 points will normally produce game. (For a minor suit game 29 points will be required.)

33 points will normally produce a small slam.

37 points will normally produce a grand slam.

Opening Bids of 1 in a Suit

In opening bids of 1 in a suit the value of a hand is determined by computing the high cards held and adding:

3 points for a void

2 points for each singleton

1 point for each doubleton

13 point hands are optional openings. Bid them if convenient.

14 point hands *must* be opened.

A third hand opening may be made with 11 points, or even a little less, if a fairly good suit is held.

Charles H. Goren's

POINT COUNT
BIDDING

IN CONTRACT BRIDGE

♠ ♡ ◇ ♣ ♠ ♡ ◇ ♣ ♠ ♡ ◇ ♣ ♠ ♡ ◇ ♣ ♠ ♡ ◇ ♣

SIMON AND SCHUSTER
NEW YORK

REVISED EDITION—27TH PRINTING, OCTOBER, 1961

MANUFACTURED IN THE UNITED STATES OF AMERICA
BY J. W. CLEMENT CO., BUFFALO, NEW YORK

TABLE OF CONTENTS

Foreword 7

I. Opening Bids of 1 in a Suit 9

II. Opening 2 Bids 21

III. Opening Pre-emptive Bids 25

IN BRIEF 26

IV. The Point Count As It Applies to
No Trump Bidding 27

V. Responses to No Trump Bids 31

VI. The Gerber 4 Club Convention 41

IN BRIEF 43

VII. A Few General Hints on the Valuation Table 45

VIII. Bidding with a Part Score 48

IX. Responses to Bids of 1 in a Suit 53

X. Free Bids 69

XI. Responses to 2 Bids 73

IN BRIEF 78

XII. Rebids by Opener 79

XIII. Rebids by Responder 90

XIV. Overcalls 98

XV. The Take-out Double 103

XVI. Responses to the Take-out Double 107

IN BRIEF 115

XVII. Penalty Doubles 116

Quizzes 119

Answers to Quizzes 134

A SUMMARY 151

FOREWORD

It is gratifying to report that in this new printing, in addition to the ample space so generously offered me by the publishers, I shall have available additional pages which were formerly devoted to the promotional job of selling my Point Count method to the public. The universal acceptance of these methods has rendered such build-up unnecessary, and we are devoting the extra space to the presentation of some of the newer developments in the game of Contract and to a fuller treatment of the subject by way of quizzes all of which are brand-new.

—CHARLES H. GOREN

CHAPTER I

OPENING BIDS OF 1 IN A SUIT

THE POINT COUNT TABLE

ACE = 4 POINTS

KING = 3 POINTS

QUEEN = 2 POINTS

JACK = 1 POINT

The Pack contains 40 points*

An average hand is 10 points

Unprotected honors should be discounted. Where the King is unguarded (alone) it should be reduced from 3 to 2. The unguarded Queen (Q or Qx) should be reduced from 2 to 1, and the singleton Jack should be regarded as a singleton spot card. However, the reduction should not be made in cases where partner has bid the suit.

Note that while the value of the unguarded honor changes, the distributional points always remain constant. Deduct a point for an Aceless hand. Add a point if a hand contains four Aces.

To illustrate:

		(A)
♠	A J x x x	(5)
♡	K Q x	(5)
◊	J x x x	(1)
♣	K	(2 + 2 for singleton)

The unguarded King is reduced from 3 to 2 points

*While for No Trump bidding the pack remains constant at 40 points, it will be seen that there can be no such constant figure for suit bidding.

(B)

♠ K J 10 x x	(4)
♡ A J x x	(5)
◇ K x	(3 + 1 for doubleton)
♣ Q x	(1 + 1 for doubleton)

The unguarded Queen is reduced from 2 to 1 point

(C)

♠ A Q x x x	(6)
♡ K Q x	(5)
◇ Q x x	(2)
♣ J x	(1 for doubleton)

The unguarded Jack is discounted entirely

THE VALUE of a hand for purposes of opening the bidding is computed by adding the high card point count to the *points assigned for distribution*. The points assigned for distribution are as follows:

ADD 3 POINTS FOR A VOID

ADD 2 POINTS FOR EACH SINGLETON

ADD 1 POINT FOR EACH DOUBLETON

Requirements

If your hand contains 13 points you have an optional opening bid, and you may open if you feel like it. Be sure, however, that your hand contains at least two quick (defensive) tricks.

If your hand contains 14 points it must be opened!

Since the allowance of value for short suits in the opening hand will appear to be a departure from long established theories, let us examine briefly how it works.

♠ A K J x x (8)
♡ A x x   (4)
◇ x x x
♣ x x   (1)

This hand contains only 13 points but since it has a convenient rebid of 2 Spades it should be opened. It will be noted that a point is allowed for the doubleton Club. This produces the same result as though a point had been allowed instead for the fifth Spade, a practice which has been followed by most writers who have previously written on the point count. If the result appears to be the same, why then, the reader may ask, do I use a different method?

The answer is simple: by counting only the fifth and sixth card of your long suit certain distributional advantages are completely lost. Take these two hands:

(A) ♠ A K J x x   (B) ♠ A K J x x
    ♡ A x x   ♡ A x x x
    ◇ x x x   ◇ x x
    ♣ x x   ♣ x x

Which one is better? Definitely hand (B). What is the margin of superiority? The fourth Heart, for which some writers have not made allowance. By assigning a point for each of the doubletons, we reach a value of 14 points for hand (B) compared with 13 for hand (A). What I have really done is allow a point for the fifth Spade and a point for the fourth Heart, but that would be too much work, and much too difficult to remember. It is much simpler to reach the precise answer by counting the short suits. This takes care of all distributions.

Let us see how that principle applies to four card suits:

♠ A 10 9 x (4)
♡ A x x   (4)
◇ A x x   (4)
♣ x x x

This hand contains only 12 points and should be passed.

♠ A 10 9 x (4)
♡ A x x   (4)
◇ x x   (1)
♣ A 10 x x (4)

This hand contains 13 points and is an optional opening. The opening bid of 1 Club is recommended because an easy rebid of 1 Spade is available over partner's expected response of 1 in a suit.

♠ A 10 x x (4)
♡ A 10 x x (4)
◇ x   (2)
♣ A x x x (4)

This hand contains 14 points and must be opened.

It will be seen that if only the fifth card in a suit is taken into consideration the following three hands would all have the same value.

(A)	(B)	(C)
♠ A 10 x x	♠ A 10 x x	♠ A 10 x x
♡ A x x	♡ A x x x	♡ A x x x
◇ A x x	◇ A x x	◇ x
♣ x x x	♣ x x	♣ A x x x
(A)—12	(B)—13	(C)—14

Let us see how this works with two suiters.

♠ A Q x x x (6)
♡ A 10 x x x (4)
◇ x x   (1)
♣ x   (2)

I think your instinct will tell you that this hand should be opened. Our experience convinces us that such action is mandatory. In high cards the hand contains only 10 points. If only the fifth Spade were taken into consideration the hand would have a value of 11 points, and would be an obvious pass. But, allowing 2 points for the singleton and 1 point for the doubleton brings the value of the hand to 13 points. Since an easy rebid of 2 Hearts is available, the hand should be opened with 1 Spade.

The soundness of this doctrine becomes apparent with a slight rearrangement of the above hand:

(A)	(B)
♠ A Q x x x	♠ A Q x x x
♡ A 10 x x x	♡ A 10 x
◇ x x	◇ x x x
♣ x	♣ x x

Hand (A) is obviously 2 points better than hand (B). Counting the singleton and doubleton has not only permitted us to reach the exact valuation for the hand, but has actually lightened our mental burden, in the sense that it did some of our thinking for us.

Notice that hand (A) undergoes no change in value if the two short suits are combined to produce a void suit, e.g.,

♠ A Q x x x (6)
♡ A 10 x x x (4)
◇ x x x
♣ none   (3)

The hand retains a value of 13 points.

Examine the following hands containing four card suits:

(A)	(B)	(C)
♠ A J x x (5)	♠ A J x x (5)	♠ A x x x (4)
♡ A K x x (7)	♡ A K x (7)	♡ K J x x (4)
◇ x x x	◇ J x x (1)	◇ x (2)
♣ x x (1)	♣ x x x	♣ K J x x (4)
——	——	——
13	13	14

Hand (A) contains 13 points which makes it an optional opening. The option in this case should be exercised because a convenient rebid is available if you open with 1 Spade. Partner responds 2 Clubs, and you are in a position conveniently to rebid 2 Hearts. Hand (B) also contains 13 points but the option to bid need not be exercised since there is no convenient rebid. Hand (C) contains 14 points and is therefore a mandatory opening of 1 Club.

To repeat, where a hand contains only one long suit the addition of 1 point for the fifth and 1 point for the sixth card will produce accurate results, but where a second suit is held such valuation will be false. Such methods will also prove faulty when three suits are held. (See Page 20 for an example of this type of hand.)

1 Club Opening

There is a common misconception that this is a system or convention. Nothing could be farther from the truth. The short Club bid is used to open the bidding on hands that contain the necessary values but offer no other convenient opening or rebid. A 1 Club opening always makes it easy to rebid for if worse comes to worst opener may rebid 1 No Trump.

(A)	
♠ A K Q x	(9)
♡ x x x	
◇ x x x	
♣ A J x	(5)
	—
	14

(B)	
♠ 10 x x x	
♡ Q 10 x x	(2)
◇ K x	(3)
♣ A K J	(8)
1 for the	
doubleton	(1)
	—
	14

Both these hands are mandatory openings. In hand (A) if you open 1 Spade, an awkward situation develops if partner responds 2 Hearts or 2 Diamonds. Therefore, bid 1 Club.

In hand (B) no good biddable suit is available so the bidding should be opened with 1 Club.

For purposes of opening the bidding with 1 of a major suit when that suit is only four cards long, the suit must contain a minimum of 4 points in high cards. Examples of biddable major suits:

A x x x
K J x x
K Q x x

Note that this requirement applies only to the opening bid; it does not refer to the responder nor to the opening bidder when he is making a rebid.

Third Position Openings

In third position, the bidding may be opened with as little as 11 points. In fact, with an understanding partner, I may shade the requirements to 10 points where a good suit is held. The reason for relaxing the requirements is that the third hand opener is not required to make a rebid. He has a passing partner, and even if responder names a new suit, the third hand bidder need not go on.

♠ A K J x x   (8)
♡ Q x x   (2)
◊ x x x
♣ x x   (1)
—
11

This hand should be opened in third position with a bid of 1 Spade.

Opening bidder, in this case, need not bid again, for it is reasonable to presume that a passing bidder will not contribute 14 points, so that the partnership cannot have the 26 points needed for game.

But he should be prepared to cope with partner's response, even if such handling involves a pass. If partner is apt to respond in a suit in which you hold a singleton, and you have no convenient rebids, it is better to pass with hands containing less than 12 points.

Fourth Position Openings

The requirements for a fourth hand opening bid are the same as for first and second hand. There is one distinction. Opener need not be prepared to rebid, inasmuch as his partner passed originally.

♠ A Q x x   (6)
♡ A K x   (7)
◊ x x x
♣ x x x
—
13

This is a good opening in fourth position (13 points), though it would not be acceptable for first or second hand, because a convenient rebid is not available.

Choice of Suits

The use of the point count for hand valuation has no effect on the established rules about which suit to bid first. The rules remain as always.

With two five card suits bid the higher ranking first (with some exceptions, where five Spades and five Clubs are held).

With a five and a four card suit bid the five card suit first. (See exceptions.)

With a six-five, bid the six card suit first, then bid the five card suit twice.

With four card suits start with the suit that ranks next below your singleton or doubleton.

EXCEPTIONS:

Treat any weak five card suit as though it were a four card suit when this will create a convenient rebid—for example:

♠ J x x x x
♡ K 10 x
♢ x
♣ A K J x

Treating the weak five card Spade suit as though it were a four card suit, it would then be proper to open with the suit below the singleton, i.e., 1 Club.

Example:

You hold:

♠ K x x x x
♡ x
♢ x x
♣ A K J x x

For the sake of convenience this hand is opened with 1 Club. A Spade opening would prove awkward if partner responds 2 Hearts or 2 Diamonds, for no convenient rebid is available. The hand is not strong enough for a rebid at the level of 3 Clubs; therefore you would find yourself in the position of having to rebid 2 Spades on a non-rebiddable suit.

Exception to the five-four rule: With hands of moderate strength, particularly where your suits are next-door-neighbors in rank, the hand should be treated as though the suits were of equal length. For example, as dealer you hold:

♠ A K J x
♡ K Q x x x
◇ x x
♣ x x

This is a hand of moderate strength and the suits are next-door-neighbors. It is better to make believe that your Spades and Hearts are the same length. Therefore, open the bidding with 1 Spade, providing an easy rebid of 2 Hearts over partner's response.

As dealer you hold:

♠ A K x x
♡ A K x x x
◇ K x
♣ x x

Here the opening bidder's hand has great strength (19 points) and should be bid naturally, that is, the five card suit first. The proper opening bid is 1 Heart. Over a bid of 2 Clubs you are well prepared to rebid 2 Spades. This is equivalent to bidding at the level of 3, which requires a good hand. This hand qualifies as such inasmuch as it is valued at 19 points, 17 in high cards and 2 for distribution (1 for each doubleton). The requirements for a reverse may occasionally be shaded to 18 points.

On three-suited hands that are valued at 20 points or more, and where the text book opening bid would be 1 Spade, it is good tactics to open exceptionally with 1 of a minor suit in order to make it easy for partner to respond, for example:

As dealer you hold:

♠ A K x x
♡ A Q x x
◇ K Q 10 x
♣ x

This hand is valued at 20 points (18 in high cards and 2 for the singleton Club). The normal opening is 1 Spade, the suit below the singleton. However, partner would not respond to a bid of 1 Spade if he held the following hand:

♠ x x
♡ K J 10 x x
◇ x x x
♣ x x x

for it possesses only 4 points in high cards and does not qualify as a 1 No Trump response.* But if the opening bid is 1 Diamond, responder may make a shaded response of 1 Heart. For purposes of bidding a suit his hand is valued at 5 points (4 in high cards and 1 for the doubleton).

EXAMPLES of long-card hands. Do not regard these values for doubletons, singletons and voids as ruffing values. On the contrary, they represent long cards. If a hand contains a doubleton, it must hold one long card; if it contains a singleton, it must hold two long cards; if it contains a void, it must hold three long cards.

Now, what are long cards? You start counting your long cards from the fifth card of the trump suit and the fourth card of any side suit. For example:

*See page 53 on responses.

(A)	(B)
♠ A K x x x	♠ A x x x
♡ A x x x	♡ x
◇ x x x	◇ A K J x
♣ x	♣ K x x x

On hand (A) the opening bid is 1 Spade. It is worth 13 points, 11 points in high cards, one for the fifth Spade (trumps) and one for the fourth Heart (a side suit).

On hand (B) the opening bid is 1 Diamond. It is worth 17 points, 15 points in high cards and two for distribution—1 for the fourth Spade (a side suit), 1 for the fourth Club (a side suit), but no point is assigned for length in Diamonds. That is the trump suit, and we count length in the trump suit only from the fifth card.

When I first presented this technique to the public in 1949, this was the method employed, that is, counting long cards. Students were told to add 1 point for each trump over four, and 1 point for each card over three in any side suit. This was the Rule of 3 and 4.

You may have observed how cumbersome it is to count these long cards. My students found it so, and since exactly the same result is obtained by adding 1 point for each doubleton, 2 points for each singleton and 3 points for a void, I substituted the simpler formula, which was universally accepted throughout the country and has now become standard.

CHAPTER II

OPENING 2 BIDS

ONE of the gratifying things about the presentation of this point count is that I am in a position to offer a cure for a malady that has been ravaging Bridge communities for almost two decades. I refer to the epidemic type of 2 demand bids. To say that this convention is generally abused is to put it with extreme mildness. And the ailment knows no geographical boundaries. From under the shadow of the Empire State Building to the Yosemite Valley you will find players bursting into a 2 demand bid any time they catch a glimpse of anything resembling 5½ quick tricks.

From time to time various formulae have been prescribed for the player who prefers not to think it out for himself. In the early, uninformed days of Contract the price was fixed at 5½ honor tricks and a biddable suit. That's the one that did all the damage, and it left its mark for another generation.

Then came the formula that read, "You must have more honor tricks than losers." This seemed confusing.

Then followed the rule of 13, which I never quite mastered.

But despite all these one still heard "The Song of the 2 Bid." I don't know how the tune runs but the lyrics have fastened themselves in my memory. Here's the opening line of the chorus: "I can't understand it, partner; I had 5½ honor tricks."

My own formula was perhaps the simplest of all. You must have game in hand (almost). That is to say, if you open 2

Spades, you should be able to win at least nine tricks in your own hand, and your hand must contain at least four high card tricks. This, I believe, was the most successful of all in bringing light to the community.

It was easy to use on solid hands such as:

♠ A K Q J x x x
♡ A x
◇ x
♣ A x x

but a little more difficult on hands with scattered strength; like this:

♠ A K J x x
♡ A
◇ A K x
♣ K Q 10 x

It has been suggested that the point count is of no practical use for 2 bids. This I must deny vehemently, for we have it now. There is good reason to be confident that the current formula will put an end to the sewing circle 2 bid. A student following this method can hardly go wrong. The point count actually does some of his thinking for him.

The requirements for an opening 2 demand bid are in brief as follows:

A. With a good five card suit, above 25 points

B. With a good six card suit, about 23 points

C. With a good seven card suit, about 21 points

D. With a second good five card suit, 1 point less than above

See how this works:

(A)	
♠ A K J x x	(8)
♡ A	(4)
◇ A K x	(7)
♣ K Q 10 x	(5)
2 for singleton	(2)
	—
	26

(B)	
♠ A K Q J x x	(10)
♡ A K x	(7)
◇ A x	(4)
♣ x x	
1 for each doubleton	(2)
	—
	23

(C)	
♠ A K Q J x x x	(10)
♡ A x	(4)
◇ x	
♣ A x x	(4)
2 for the singleton	
1 for the doubleton	(3)
	—
	21

Open 2 Spades on all these hands.

(A) A good 5 card suit with 26 points

(B) A good 6 card suit with 23 points

(C) A good 7 card suit with 21 points

This will shield the student from the temptation of opening with a two bid on the following hand:

♠ A Q x x x	(6)
♡ A K x	(7)
◇ A K x	(7)
♣ x x	
1 for doubleton	(1)
	—
	21

This hand, it will be seen, has the value of only 21 points and does not approach an opening two demand bid. It should be opened with 1 Spade, and if partner does not keep the bidding open do not be concerned about having missed a game.

When opening with a 2 bid, it is discreet to assume that partner is trickless, or virtually so. Accordingly, if you have any insufficiently guarded honors in short suits, it is sound practice not to count them, since you must assume that they will fall to opponent's high cards. Holdings like J x or Q x had better be discounted entirely when contemplating a 2 demand bid.

The requirements for 2 bids as stated above assume that there is a good chance that the hand is to be played in a major suit or No Trump. If it seems that your hand must play in a minor suit, the requirements should be increased by 2 points.

Conversely, where you have a good major two suiter, you may occasionally relax the requirements by a point or two.

CHAPTER III

OPENING PRE-EMPTIVE BIDS

OPENING pre-emptive bids are not made with good hands. Their sole purpose is to discommode the enemy. Any hand containing more than two quick tricks should not be opened with a pre-empt. To put it in another way: Do not pre-empt on any hand that contains more than 10 points in high cards (exclusive of distribution).

The following hands may be opened with pre-emptive bids of 3 Spades:

♠ K Q J 10 x x x x	♠ Q J 10 x x x x x
♡ x x	♡ x x
◇ x x	◇ A x
♣ x	♣ x

In fact, when not vulnerable, good results may be obtained by opening such hands with 4 Spades. They each possess 7 winners, safeguarding the opener against any great disaster.

IN BRIEF

The value of a hand is determined by computing the high cards held, and adding:

   3 points for a void
   2 points for each singleton
   1 point for each doubleton

---

13 point hands are optional openings. Bid them if convenient.
14 point hands must be opened.

A third hand opening may be made with 11 points if a fairly good suit is held.
A fourth hand opening should be made on 13 points, even though no good rebid is available.

An opening demand bid of 2 in a suit requires:
A good five card suit with a minimum of 25 points
A good six card suit with a minimum of 23 points
A good seven card suit with a minimum of 21 points

Do not make an opening pre-emptive bid on any hand containing more than 10 points (exclusive of distribution).

CHAPTER IV

THE POINT COUNT AS IT APPLIES TO NO TRUMP BIDDING

OPENING NO TRUMP BIDS

ACE = 4 POINTS

KING = 3 POINTS

QUEEN = 2 POINTS

JACK = 1 POINT

The Pack contains 40 points

With hands containing all four Aces, add 1 point.

IT IS highly desirable to keep this figure 40 constant. It is for this reason that it is better practice, in No Trump, not to assign points for distribution; for if each partner does so, a deal might contain as many as 76 points. The advantage of retaining the 40 points as a constant is this: When you can count your assets to 37, you know for a certainty that the opposition cannot hold an Ace, for they have only 3 points between them.

However, I do recognize the value of a five card suit, but I obtain distributional values by a slightly different approach. A raise from 1 No Trump to 2 No Trump requires 8 points; but you may raise with 7 points if you have a reasonably good five card suit or if you have good intermediate cards.

A raise from 1 No Trump to 3 No Trump requires 10 points, but you may do it with 9 if you have a five card suit. It's just as easy and keeps the numbers even. To put it in another way: with five card suits the requirements for raises and rebids are lowered by a point.

---

26 points will normally produce 3 No Trump

33 points will normally produce 6 No Trump

37 points will normally produce 7 No Trump

OPENING 1 NO TRUMP BIDS

The requirements for an open 1 No Trump bid are:
(1) The point count must be between 16 and 18
(2) The hand must be balanced, that is

4-3-3-3
4-4-3-2
5-3-3-2

with the proviso that the doubleton should be headed by a high honor
(3) At least three suits must be protected
Hands counting 19, 20 and 21 are too big for 1 No Trump and must be opened with 1 of a suit. On the second round opener will make a jump rebid in No Trump.

The question is frequently raised, why are hands counting 19, 20 and 21 too big for 1 No Trump? The reason is to be found in our requirements for raises. If your partner opens with 1 No Trump and you have a balanced hand, 8 points are required for a raise. If you have only 6 or 7, you should pass.

If partner has opened 1 No Trump with 20 or 21 points

and you have passed with 6 or 7, the partnership may possess as many as 28 points; yet the hand will be played in 1 No Trump. If the opening bid, instead, is 1 of a suit, partner will respond at the level of 1 with as little as 6 points. Opener may then jump in No Trump, knowing that the partnership probably has the necessary 26 points.

Not infrequently I have observed players making a 1 No Trump bid on hands like this:

♠ K Q x x
♡ A J x x
♢ A
♣ K x x x

"I had 17 points," they announce, as though standing upon their rights.

A 1 No Trump opening must not only have the right SIZE, but it must have the right SHAPE.

No Trump openings *must* be made on a balanced hand, that is: 4-3-3-3 — 4-4-3-2 — 5-3-3-2. Never on 4-4-4-1.

Opening Bid of 2 No Trump

The requirements for an opening bid of 2 No Trump are:
(1) The point count must be between 22 and 24
(2) The hand must be balanced in distribution
(3) All four suits must be protected
An opening bid of 2 No Trump is not forcing. Partner may pass if he lacks the necessary values to raise.

Opening Bid of 3 No Trump

The requirements for an opening bid of 3 No Trump are:
(1) The point count must be between 25 and 27
(2) The hand must be balanced in distribution
(3) All four suits must be protected

Hands containing 28 and 29 points are too strong for an opening bid of 3 No Trump and may be opened with a bid of 4 No Trump.

Hands with 30 or more points must be opened with a 2 demand bid even though it involves doing so with a four card suit.

CHAPTER V

RESPONSES TO NO TRUMP BIDS

CONSTANTLY bear in mind that it takes approximately 26 points to make a game at No Trump. When a five card suit is held, 25 points will usually be sufficient.

Permit me to inject a cheerful note by reminding you that 33 or 34 points will normally produce a small slam. (Opponents cannot have two Aces,' since their high card strength is limited to 7 points.) And I trust that it will be of more than academic interest to you that 37 or 38 should yield a grand slam. (Opponents cannot have an Ace, since their maximum high card holding is 3 points.)

In many cases responder can tell at a glance what the total partnership assets amount to. This is done by simple arithmetic. For the opener, by his opening bid of 1 No Trump, 2 No Trump, or 3 No Trump, has announced almost exactly how many points he has.

Responding to an
Opening Bid of 1 No Trump

When responder holds a balanced hand

When partner opens with 1 No Trump and you have a 5-3-3-2, there is no advantage in showing your suit. Raise the No Trump if you have the required count.

Raise to 2 No Trump with 8 or 9 points. (You may raise with 7 points if you have a five card suit.)

Raise to 3 No Trump with 10 to 14 points.

Raise to 4 No Trump with 15 or 16 points.

Raise to 6 No Trump with 17 or 18 points.

If you hold 19 or 20 points, a bid of 6 No Trump is not quite adequate. First make a jump shift to 3 of some suit, and then follow up with 6 No Trump. Showing a suit and jumping to 6 No Trump is a little stronger action than just jumping to 6 No Trump.

Raise to 7 No Trump with 21 or more, for then your partnership is assured of at least 37 points.

When responder holds an unbalanced hand

The methods formerly in vogue for handling responses to opening No Trump bids with unbalanced hands have had to be changed somewhat to conform with our modern theories of the game.

Of all the methods that have been tried in recent years, the only one that has successfully passed the test of practical experience is the so called "2-Club Convention."

Where responder has a holding which might lend itself to suit play rather than No Trump, he conducts a preliminary examination by means of the 2-Club take-out. It will frequently be found that where each of the partners has four cards of a major suit, the hand may play to better advantage at a suit contract.

Let us examine a few hands to illustrate the current treatment.

(A)	♠ KQ43	(B)	♠ K1042	(C)	♠ AJ1063
	♡ A1075		♡ 75		♡ K85
	◇ J632		◇ K863		◇ 964
	♣ 7		♣ K92		♣ 102

With each of the foregoing hands the correct response is 2 Clubs. This is a purely artificial bid having nothing to do with the Club suit itself, and shows a minimum of 8 high card points and a holding of at least four cards in one of the major suits. It is unconditionally forcing for one round and asks the opening bidder to show a biddable major suit (Q x x x or better) if he has one.

Hand (A) contains the values for a direct raise to 3 No Trump. However, since a suit contract may prove superior with this unbalanced holding, responder wishes to probe for a possible fit in one of the majors. If he bids a major suit himself, that will show a five card suit, so he resorts to the artificial bid and partner's response will indicate whether or not there is a major suit fit.

The responses are as follows: With a biddable major the opener shows it; if he has both 4 Spades and 4 Hearts, he bids Spades first; in the event that he has no major suit he bids 2 Diamonds. This is an artificial bid and has no relationship to his holding in Diamonds.

If responder's 2 Club bid on hand (A) elicits a reply in Hearts or Spades, responder will, of course, raise to game. If the opener bids 2 Diamonds denying either major, responder investigates no further but jumps to 3 No Trump, inasmuch as he is able to count the required 26 points. Note that he does not bid 2 No Trump which would not be forcing.

On hands (B) and (C) responder has the ingredients for a raise to 2 No Trump. But in each instance it is desirable to investigate the possibilities of a suit contract on the way. On hand (B) if opener's rebid over 2 Clubs is 2 Spades, responder will raise to 4. Over 2 Hearts or 2 Diamonds he will return to 2 No Trump. This bid is not forcing and opener should pass if he has a bare 16 points, since responder would have contracted for game himself if he had 10 points.

Similarly on hand (C), if opener shows a Spade suit responder will raise to 3. If opener bids 2 Diamonds or 2 Hearts, responder can now bid 2 Spades himself. This call is not forcing and opener should pass unless he has more than a minimum or a fit in Spades. With anything above 16 points he can either rebid No Trump or raise the Spades, depending upon the nature of his holding.

The inauguration of the 2-Club Convention changes the status of the other 2 level suit responses to the opening No Trump. A bid of 2 Diamonds, 2 Hearts or 2 Spades is employed to denote an unbalanced hand of less than 8 points with a five card suit. For example, if your partner opened with 1 No Trump and you held:

♠ K J x x x   ♡ x   ◇ x x x x   ♣ x x x

it would be proper for you to respond 2 Spades. Partner is expected to pass this bid since with a good hand you would either have jumped in Spades or else employed the 2-Club Convention.

Take-out to 3 of a Suit

Where responder's hand contains the high card values for a raise to 3 No Trump (that is, at least 10 points) and also contains a long suit, a jump in that suit may be given, e.g.,

Partner opens 1 No Trump. You hold:

♠ K Q x x x
♡ x
◇ A J x x
♣ x x x

Your hand contains the high card requirements for a jump to 3 No Trump, but a jump to 3 Spades is preferable.

Again partner opens 1 No Trump. You hold:

♠ x
♡ A J x x
◊ K Q x x x x
♣ x x

Respond with 3 Diamonds. This is the equivalent of contracting for game in No Trump, but it has one additional advantage: opener may have had a four card Heart suit and the 3 Diamond bid will afford opener the chance to bid 3 Hearts. If he goes on to 3 No Trump, of course you relax. There is, therefore, not much to be gained by employing the 2 Club response on this hand.

Take-out to 4 of a Major

This is done with a hand containing a long suit (at least six cards) but less than 10 points in high cards. Responder should expect to win about five tricks in his own hand.

Partner opens 1 No Trump. You hold:

♠ x
♡ K J 10 x x x x
◊ x x x
♣ x x

Respond 4 Hearts, which opener must pass. This is not at all drastic because when it is considered that the Heart suit has been supported (the No Trump bid obviously implied Heart support), your hand is worth 12 points. Its original valuation is 7 points, to which are added 1 point for the fifth, 2 for the sixth, and 2 for the seventh Heart. You therefore have ample points for a game contract.

Rebids by Opening No Trumper
When Responder Bids 2 Diamonds,
2 Hearts or 2 Spades

The opening No Trump bidder is not expected to take drastic action of his own volition. He has presumably told his whole story on the opening bid, and all display of heroism should be left to his partner. That's why there is no such bidding as:

Opener	Responder
1 No Trump	2 Hearts
3 No Trump	

There are several instances where opener MUST pass.

(a) When responder bids 3 No Trump

(b) When responder bids 4 Hearts or 4 Spades

(c) When responder raises to 2 No Trump and opener has a minimum No Trump bid of 16 points

(d) When responder bids 2 Diamonds, 2 Hearts or 2 Spades and opener has 16 or 17 points and no good fit for partner's suit.

When responder has bid 2 Diamonds, and partner has a near maximum No Trump, which includes 2 high honors in responder's suit (A K x, A Q x, or K Q x), he should raise to 3 of the minor. This bid responder is at liberty to pass, but occasionally responder will be in position to go on to 3 No Trump with a relatively weak hand, when he is assured that his six or seven card suit is established, e.g.,

North—♠ x   ♡ Kxx   ◇ Q10xxxx   ♣ xxx
South—♠ QJx   ♡ Axx   ◇ AKx   ♣ KJxx

South bids 1 No Trump. North responds 2 Diamonds, announcing an unbalanced hand that is weak in high cards. South, who has a near maximum No Trump, including two of the top honors in Diamonds, raises to 3. North may pass if he chooses, but knowing that his partner has the Ace and King of Diamonds, which will probably permit the cashing of 6 tricks in that suit, he may take a chance on 3 No Trump.

Similarly, when the response has been 2 Hearts or 2 Spades, and the opener has a maximum No Trump, with a good fit in the responder's suit, he may raise to 3, but never to 4. If the responder has a reasonable hand, he will proceed to game himself, e.g.,

North—♠ KQ10xx   ♡ x   ◇ xxxxx   ♣ xx
South—♠ AJxx   ♡ Kxxx   ◇ Ax   ♣ AQx

South opens with 1 No Trump and North responds 2 Spades. South's hand revalues to 19 points in support of Spades so he now offers a raise to 3. Since North has a near maximum for his original bid he proceeds to 4 Spades.

Responses to Opening Bids of 2 No Trump (With Balanced Hands)

Always add your points to those shown by partner's opening.

With 4 to 8 points raise to 3 No Trump. You know there is no slam, since the most partner can have is 24 points (24 + 8 = 32).

With 9 points raise to 4 No Trump. There may be a slam, if partner has a maximum of 24 points (24 + 9 = 33).

With 10 points there will be a slam unless partner has a minimum (22 points). Therefore, first bid a suit and then raise to 4 No Trump. Bidding a suit and raising to 4 No Trump is stronger than just bidding 4 No Trump.

With 11 or 12 points bid 6 No Trump. You have at least 33 points if partner has a minimum of 22 ($22 + 11 = 33$) and at most you have 36 if partner has a maximum of 24 ($24 + 12 = 36$).

With 13 or 14 points first bid a suit and then bid 6 No Trump. This is stronger than just bidding 6 No Trump directly. It asks partner to bid 7 if he has a maximum.

With 15 points you may bid 7 No Trump. No checking for Aces is necessary, for opponents cannot have one if partner has bid correctly ($22 + 15 = 37$). Opponents have at most 3 points.

(With Unbalanced Hands)

(1) Bid any six card major suit regardless of the high card content of your hand.

(2) Bid any five card major suit if your hand contains at least 4 points in high cards.
(This may be shaded to 3 points with a highly unbalanced hand.)

(3) Jump to 4 in a major suit with a six card suit and a hand containing about 7 points in high cards.

(4) With 4 points or more and at least one four card major suit, bid 3 Clubs. This bid asks partner to show a major suit, or to bid 3 Diamonds if he does not have one.

Examples:

Partner opens with 2 No Trump. You hold:

(A)	(B)
♠ K 10 x x x	♠ 10 9 x x x x x
♡ Q x x	♡ x
◇ x	◇ x x x
♣ x x x x	♣ x x

(C)	(D)
♠ K J 10 x x x	♠ K x x x
♡ x	♡ x x
◇ x x	◇ x x x
♣ K x x x	♣ K x x x

(E)

♠ K Q 10 x x x
♡ x
◇ x x
♣ K 10 9 8

(A) Bid 3 Spades. If partner rebids 3 No Trump or 4 Spades, pass. With only 5 points in high cards, no slam is to be visualized. But the hand may play better in Spades.

(B) Bid 3 Spades. If partner bids 3 No Trump, bid 4 Spades. This hand must play in Spades and you arrange to do so by bidding Spades one at a time at the cheapest possible level. Do not make the mistake of jumping to 4 Spades.

(C) Bid 4 Spades. This shows a six card suit with enough high cards to produce a slam opposite a maximum 2 No Trump bid. You have 7 points in high cards, which with a six card suit is a very impressive holding.

(D) Bid 3 Clubs, a one round force, asking partner to show a major suit. If partner bids 3 Spades, you will raise to 4, if he bids 3 Diamonds or 3 Hearts, you will return to No Trump.

(E) Jump to 5 Spades. This is almost a sure slam.

Responses to Opening Bids of
3 No Trump

Remember partner has 25 to 27, keep your eye on the figures 33 (small slam) and 37 (grand slam).

With a five card major suit and 7 points in high cards, show that suit.

♠ A J x x x
♡ Q x x
◇ x x x
♣ x x

Bid 4 Spades.

With 7 points and no five card suit bid 4 No Trump.

With 8 or 9 points bid 6 No Trump. You have at least 33 and at most 36.

With 10 or 11 points bid 4 Diamonds,* and then rebid 6 No Trump on the next round. Partner should bid 7 with a maximum opening. Showing a suit and then bidding 6 No Trump is stronger than a direct leap to 6 No Trump.

With 12 points bid 7 No Trump. No checking for Aces is necessary. Opponents can't have one (25+12=37).

---

*The Diamond bid is really artificial—4 of a major cannot be employed in this situation because opener may pass; and 4 Clubs is used as a conventional asking bid (The Gerber Convention). See Chapter VI.

THE GERBER 4 CLUB CONVENTION

SOMETIMES a grand slam can be made with a great many points less than the normal 37, when responder holds a very long suit.

In cases of that kind, of course, it will be desirable to check on Aces—since the opposition may have as many as 10 points. At such times the Gerber Convention (4 Clubs) will be useful.

Your partner opens 1 No Trump and you hold:

♠ x
♡ x x
◇ A K Q x x x x x
♣ A x

You know that you will play for at least 6 Diamonds but if partner has the key cards you can make a grand slam. It is possible that partner has a maximum No Trump but lacks one of the Aces. For example he might hold:

♠ K Q x
♡ A Q J
◇ J x x
♣ K Q x x

In order to determine this you burst into 4 Clubs (The Gerber Convention). This is a request for Aces. If partner shows two Aces and two Kings you may contract for 7 No Trump. Even if he shows two Aces and only one King you may, if you choose, take the reasonable risk that he has a Queen with one of his Kings and bid 7 anyhow.

A sudden burst from 1 or 2 No Trump to 4 Clubs is an artificial bid and is treated in the Blackwood manner as a request for Aces. The responses are:

4 Diamonds	—	No Aces or 4 Aces
4 Hearts	—	1 Ace
4 Spades	—	2 Aces
4 No Trump	—	3 Aces

The 4 Club bidder may then ask for Kings by calling 5 Clubs. The responses are similar to the call for Aces; with no Kings the responder bids 5 Diamonds; with 1 King, 5 Hearts; etc.

If the 4 Club bidder bids anything other than 5 Clubs over his partner's response to the call for Aces, it is a sign-off and the opener is requested to pass.

Let's suppose in response to the 4 Club bid opener called 4 Spades showing 2 Aces. If the 4 Club bidder now bids 4 No Trump that expresses a desire to play the hand at that denomination. If the 4 Club bidder had wished to ask for Kings he would have bid 5 Clubs.

─────────── IN BRIEF ───────────

26 points will normally produce game.
33 points will normally produce a small slam.
37 points will normally produce a grand slam.

───────

Opening 1 No Trump—16 to 18 points
Opening 2 No Trump—22 to 24 points
Opening 3 No Trump—25 to 27 points

───────

Responses to Opening 1 No Trump Bids:

Raise to 2 No Trump with 8 or 9 points (or 7 points with a good five card suit)
Raise to 3 No Trump with 10 to 14 points
Raise to 4 No Trump with 15 or 16 points
Raise to 6 No Trump with 17 or 18 points
Bid 3 of a suit, then 6 No Trump with 19 or 20 points
Raise to 7 No Trump with 21 points
A response of 2 Clubs shows at least 8 points in high cards and a four card major suit, and asks the opener to show a four card major if he has one.
A response of 2 Diamonds, 2 Hearts or 2 Spades contains less than 8 points, but shows a five card suit and an unbalanced hand.
A response of 4 Spades or 4 Hearts shows a long suit (six or seven cards) with less than 10 points in high cards
A response of 3 in any suit shows a hand with 10 or more points and a good suit

IN BRIEF

Responses to 2 No Trump Bids:

Raise to 3 No Trump with 4 to 8 points
Raise to 4 No Trump with 9 points
Bid 3 of a suit, then 4 No Trump with 10 points
Raise to 6 No Trump with 11 or 12 points
Bid 3 of a suit, then 6 No Trump, with 13 or 14 points
Raise to 7 No Trump with 15 points
With a five card major suit headed by an honor, and 4
    points, bid that suit at the level of 3
Show any six card major suit
Bid 3 Clubs with 4 points and a four card major suit.
    This bid asks partner to show a four card major if
    he has one.

Responses to 3 No Trump Bids:

Raise to 4 No Trump with 7 points
Raise to 6 No Trump with 8 or 9 points
Bid 4 Diamonds, then 6 No Trump with 10 or 11
    points
Raise to 7 No Trump with 12 points
Show any five card suit if the hand contains 7 points
    in high cards

CHAPTER VII

A FEW GENERAL HINTS
ON THE VALUATION TABLE

IT WILL BE observed that in all No Trump situations I have
given precise limits where one bid ends and another begins.
Because the danger of duplication is minimized, such pre-
cision is possible. But in suit bidding I have made no pretense at this type of accuracy. You will note that the top
limit of one bid is also considered the lower limit of the next
bid, e.g., in valuing your hand for the purpose of responding
to partner's opening bid of 1 in a suit, the following table
is submitted:

6-10 Mediocre hand (worth only one bid)
10-13 Fairly good hand (worth two bids)
13-16 Very good hand. Responder should insist upon game
16-19 Powerful hand, worth more than a mere game force
19 & up Slam zone. Jump shift is indicated.

You will see that hands counting 10, 13, 16, and 19 points
may be placed in one category or the other. They are the
JUDGMENT POINTS. That is to say, in these cases you
use your own judgment. Put them in the upper bracket if
you feel bullish; in the lower bracket if you feel bearish. In
this respect I am not merely consulting your whims. There are
various factors that may properly induce an optimistic or a
pessimistic attitude. It is perhaps needless to say that the
point count is not a substitute for thinking.

Nor has any pretense been made for the infallibility of
the point count method. Just as the honor trick table had its

imperfections, the point count has certain slight defects which I feel it my duty to point out to you. When a hand possesses certain flaws a deduction of 1 point should be made in the count.

A hand without an Ace is considered to possess a flaw in the case of the opening bidder.

$$
\begin{array}{lll}
\spadesuit & K\,Q\,x & (5) \\
\heartsuit & K\,Q\,x & (5) \\
\diamondsuit & Q\,J\,x\,x\,x & (3) \\
\clubsuit & x\,x & (1)
\end{array}
$$

On the surface this hand counts 14 points and would therefore be a mandatory opening. However, the hand is Aceless, a flaw for which there should be 1 point deduction. So that this hand is not an obligatory opening, and you may exercise your option to pass.

A hand with less than two quick tricks is considered to possess a flaw, in the case of the opening bidder. The quick tricks are briefly:

$$
\begin{array}{ll}
A\,K & (2) \\
A\,Q & (1\frac{1}{2}) \\
A & (1) \\
K\,Q & (1) \\
K\,x & (\frac{1}{2})
\end{array}
$$

Any hand that contains an insufficiently guarded honor is considered to possess a flaw. A doubleton Jack or a Queen, unaccompanied by another honor (Q x or J x), is obviously not as impressive as a Queen or a Jack in association with another face card (K Q x or Q J x). Now here is where your judgment comes in. Where part of your count is made up of scattered Jacks or Queens, and you have reached one of these judgment points, exercise your discretion by placing these hands in the lower bracket.

A recent publication quoted a heckler as confronting us with the following hand:

♠ Q J
♡ Q J 10 x x
◇ Q J x
♣ Q J x

Inasmuch as it counted 13 points he demanded that we open it, which we refused to do. In the first place, 13 points is only an optional opening. Secondly, this hand is not worth 13 points. It is Aceless, which calls for the deduction of 1 point. It possesses unguarded honors in Spades. Furthermore, it lacks the required two defensive tricks.

The following insufficiently guarded holdings should be viewed with suspicion unless partner has already bid the suit.

A J alone   K J alone
K Q alone   Q x
Q J alone   J x

When borderline situations present themselves, hands containing the above combinations had better be treated in the conservative manner. In other words, whenever these hands count up to one of the judgment points, it is well to place them in the lower bracket.

CHAPTER VIII

BIDDING WITH A PART SCORE

BIDDING principles, both offensive and defensive, must be modified to a degree when either side has a part score.

Under normal circumstances, a new suit by responder forces the opener to make one more bid. But where responder's call completes a game contract, the opener need not speak again. Opener, with a part score of 40, bids 1 Spade. Partner responds 2 Hearts. Opener may pass, since a game contract has been reached. If responder wishes to be assured of another chance to bid, he must make a jump shift, which is forcing for one round.

An opening 2 demand bid remains a complete force, no matter what the score, and responder is compelled to speak, even with a bust. In that case, having made his 2 No Trump denial response, he need not speak again, unless opener makes a jump rebid in a new suit, in which case he is forced for one more round.

A somewhat liberal attitude should be assumed by a responder who holds a 60 part score when partner opens the bidding with 1 of a suit. Since the contract of 1 No Trump will complete the game, he should be willing to keep the bidding open with a little less than the required points. A 1 No Trump response may then be made with only 5 points.

A part score may have some bearing on the question of opening the bidding; but part scores of 20 or 30 should be virtually ignored. Where an advanced part score is held, however, the necessity for opener's rebidding may be ignored;

48

for in most cases partner's response will complete the game contract.

Examine the following case:

♠ A Q x   ♡ A Q J x   ◇ x x x   ♣ x x x

With no part score, dealer has little choice but to pass. The hand is worth 13 points; but an immediate crisis would develop if you opened with 1 Heart, and partner responded with 2 of a minor. A pass is therefore clearly indicated. But with 60 on score, an opening bid of 1 Heart is mandatory; for you are in a position to pass a response of 2 Diamonds or 2 Clubs.

It is fundamental in our system that the use of the "short Club" bid to initiate the bidding be strictly banned when an advanced part score is held. You hold the following hand:

♠ A K 10 x   ♡ A x x   ◇ x x x   ♣ K x x

At a love score it would be bad practice to open with 1 Spade, for no suitable rebid is available over a response of 2 in a suit. It is therefore necessary to open with 1 Club to provide for a convenient rebid of 1 Spade over partner's response. With a part score however, a Club opening is not to be considered. Bid 1 Spade, intending to drop any response by partner (except a jump shift).

Even though it is not necessary to bid again, once game has been completed, occasionally opener, holding considerable excess values, should speak once more (in a mild manner) to allow for the possibility of a slam. For example, with a part score of 90 you open with 1 Diamond, holding:

♠ A x x x   ♡ x   ◇ A K J x x   ♣ Q 10 x

Partner responds with 1 Spade. With a discreet partner, my recommendation is a raise to 2 Spades. Perhaps such practice is to be avoided opposite a partner who is apt to react violently on the ground, "You overbid game and therefore are inviting a slam." This is an improper interpretation of the raise. The single raise in this case should be read, "Partner, I am offering you a raise just in case. All that I promise you is a good substantial raise."

Responder, for example, might have:

♠ K J x x x x   ♥ A x x   ♦ x   ♣ K x x

in which case he could hardly do more than respond with 1 Spade; yet after a single raise he could set out to explore slam possibilities.

Requirements for a jump shift may be relaxed to some extent when a part score is held, and it is not necessary to adhere strictly to the 19 point rule when a good fit is apparent.

Partner opens 1 Diamond, and you hold:

♠ A K 10 9 x x   ♥ x x   ♦ A J x x   ♣ x

At a clear score, a 1 Spade response would be in order. With 90 on score, however, a 2 Spade response (forcing for one round) is recommended because of the very fine fit. You naturally intend to show the Diamond fit on the next round. But if you held:

♠ A K 10 9 x x   ♥ A J x x   ♦ x   ♣ x x

a 2 Spade response is not to be considered, for if partner takes no action over 1 Spade, slam chances may be ignored.

When the adversaries have a part score, many players shy away from opening the bidding on the theory that such an act will tend to "stir up the animals." In my view, this is simply burying your head in the sand to avoid detection. If they have anything resembling a bid, they will almost surely open, and if you have the type of holding with which it may be difficult to contest at a higher level, it behooves you to get aboard early in an effort to build up your defense.

Holding the following:

♠ A K x x   ♡ A x x x   ◊ x x x   ♣ x x

we would pass at a clear score, but would open 1 Spade against an enemy part score.

It has been pointed out that a 2 demand bid with a part score is forcing for one round. It should also be pointed out that the requirements may be lowered to the extent of one playing trick. Whereas, normally a 2 bid in a major suit should be based on nine winners, in this case a 2 bid may be made on some hands containing only eight winners, provided they contain the necessary four high card tricks.

With a part score, the following are acceptable opening 2 bids:

♠ A K Q J x x   ♡ x   ◊ A x x x   ♣ A x (21)
♠ K Q J 10 x x x   ♡ A x   ◊ x   ♣ A x x (17)

When your partner opens the bidding, and you have a part score, it is not always wise to relax and permit him to run out the game. If you have a hand of definite values (perhaps the equal of an opening bid), you should take some mild action in the form of a single raise, or perhaps a 1 No Trump response, to provide for cases in which partner's hand may be just short of a demand bid. For example, with 70 on score your partner has opened with 1 Heart. You hold:

♠ x x x x   ♡ K J x   ◊ K x   ♣ A Q x x

Respond 2 Hearts, giving partner a chance to speak again. Surely any eight or nine trick contract will be safe. But you must not make the mistake of bidding 2 Clubs, for that is not now a temporizing bid. Opener may pass.

A jump raise is a more specific suggestion of slam possibilities when the bid is over game. This is a device frequently employed.

With 80 on score, partner opens 1 Heart, and you hold:

♠ J 10 9   ♡ A 10 x x   ◊ x   ♣ A K Q x x

No thought is to be given to a 2 Club response. You must choose between 3 Hearts, which is highly invitational but not forcing, and 3 Clubs, a shaded jump shift, which is forcing for one round.

Limited raises are affected by part score holdings. With 40 part score, your partner opens the bidding with 1 No Trump. You hold, let us say, 13 points. It would not be correct to jump to 3 No Trump. This would be overbidding game and would therefore be a slam invitation. Since there can be no slam, even though partner has 18 points, the proper call is 2 No Trump, completing the game. However, if you held 15 points, you would overbid the game; for, if partner had 18 points, there would be enough strength in the combined hands for slam.

CHAPTER IX

RESPONSES TO BIDS OF 1 IN A SUIT

26 Points Will Normally Produce Game

THERE'S nothing mysterious or arbitrary about this. For years I have been shouting the battle cry that AN OPENING BID FACING AN OPENING BID WILL PRODUCE GAME. It is gratifying to report that the advice has been widely heeded.

Now you are offered the point count translation of this battle cry. Let us see how this operates. The normal minimum opening bid contains about 13 points; so that when an opening bid faces an opening bid the partnership possesses about 26 points and should reach game if a convenient contract can be found.

Responding with Weak Hands

With hands of moderate strength responder may do one of three things:

(a) *Bid 1 No Trump*

This shows a balanced hand with a range of 6-10 points in high cards. (For the purpose of this response, as elsewhere in No Trump bidding, do not allow points for distribution.) Do not make this response of 1 No Trump if you are able to make a cheaper bid of 1 in a suit. This response of 1 No Trump is not forcing. IT IS A LIMIT BID.

While the upper limit of the 1 No Trump response is 10 points, as a practical matter it is wiser for opener not to rely on his partner for more than 9 points. Therefore, he should not raise to 2 No Trump with less than 17 points in high cards.

Here are two examples of hands containing the maximum 1 No Trump holding:

Partner has opened with 1 Spade. You hold:

♠ x x   ♡ K x x x   ◇ A x x   ♣ K x x x
♠ 10 x x   ♡ A x x x   ◇ K J x   ♣ Q x x

Respond 1 No Trump in each case.

(b) *Give a single raise in the suit bid*

With support for partner's suit a single raise may be given on hands ranging from 7 to 10 points. This response is not forcing. IT IS A LIMIT BID—ITS LIMIT IS 10 POINTS IN HIGH CARDS AND DISTRIBUTION.

(c) *Bid 1 in a new suit*

The minimum requirement for this is 6 points. For this purpose, since your response is in a suit, distributional points are counted.

Examples:

Partner bids 1 Heart. You hold:

> ♠ x x x
> ♡ x x
> ◇ Q x x x
> ♣ K x x x

Pass. Your hand contains only 5 points and therefore you have not sufficient values to bid 1 No Trump. For purposes of No Trump responses, the doubleton is not counted.

Partner bids 1 Heart. You hold:

> ♠ x x x
> ♡ x x
> ◇ Q x x
> ♣ K x x x x

Pass. You have only 5 points in high cards which is not enough for a 1 No Trump response.

Partner bids 1 Heart. You hold:

♠ x x x
♡ x x
◊ K x x x
♣ K x x x

Respond 1 No Trump; you have 6 points.

Partner bids 1 Heart. You hold:

♠ K x x x x
♡ x x
◊ x x x
♣ Q x x

Respond 1 Spade. Since you are making a suit response this hand is worth 6 points (5 in high cards and 1 for the doubleton). A one over one response may sometimes be shaded to 5 points including high cards and distribution.

The one over one response is not a limit bid. For, at its maximum, it may be a very powerful hand and one that is just short of a jump shift. Responder has chosen to play a waiting game. Responder assumes no risk of being dropped, for his bid is absolutely forcing for one round.

Opening bid is 1 Club. Responder holds:

(A)	(B)
♠ 10 x x x	♠ x x
♡ K Q x x	♡ A J x x x x
◊ x x x	◊ A Q x
♣ x x	♣ A x

In both cases the proper response is 1 Heart.

(A) This hand represents the minimum on which a one over one response should be made (5 points in high cards, and 1 point for the doubleton). If anyone in the audience responded 1 No Trump with this hand it is suggested that he wash out his mouth with soap and water.

(B) This hand is pretty nearly maximum. Its value is 17 points (15 points in high cards and 1 for each doubleton).

For Raises of Suit Bids

In raising partner's suit bid, one must compute the value of the hand (a) in high cards, (b) in short suits.

Naturally adequate trump support is presumed, since without normal trump support you will make some other bid in preference to raising your partner's suit.

(a) High cards are computed at their face value. However, one must have regard to the promoted value of a trump honor. Obviously the King of your partner's suit is worth more than a side King. It is a sure winner, and is the equivalent of an Ace. Similarly the Queen of partner's suit is worth more than a side Queen.

It has always been my practice to promote an honor in partner's suit to the next rank. The Ace, like the General, has no chance for advancement, and can be allotted no more than 4 points. The King of trumps, however, becomes promoted to the value of an Ace and counts 4 points; the Queen of trumps becomes promoted to the value of a King; the Jack of trumps becomes promoted to the value of a Queen.

The following are holdings in partner's suit which should be promoted:

$$K \ x \ x = 4$$
$$Q \ J \ x = 4$$
$$Q \ x \ x = 3$$
$$J \ x \ x = 2$$

However, if you have already counted at least 4 points in trumps, no promotion takes place.

The following combinations, therefore, all count at their exact face value; for you have already counted at least a full trick (4 points) in that suit, and no promotion takes place.

A K x = 7
A Q x = 6
A J x = 5
K Q x = 5
K J x = 4

For those players who find promoting honors and subtracting for only three trumps a cumbersome chore, a substitute method is suggested: calculate the value of your hand according to its face value and then subtract one point if your trump support is not quite adequate. This will eliminate both promoting and subtracting, and will produce the same result in a vast majority of cases.

(b) Short Suits:
  Add 1 point for each doubleton
  Add 3 points for each singleton
  Add 5 points for a void

(Note the difference in valuation of short suits between the opening bidder's hand and the responder's hand.)

Certain deductions are made when your hand, as prospective dummy, contains a flaw. There are three very common defects or flaws:

1. Possession of only three trumps when raising partner's suit is a flaw.

2. A 4-3-3-3 distribution is a flaw when raising partner's suit.

3. A short suit containing an insufficiently guarded honor is a flaw.

When dummy's hand is freakish, a strict adherence to point count requirements for a raise is not expected. If dummy contains five trumps, the requirements for a raise may be shaded by a point. For example, partner opens with 1 Spade and you hold:

♠ 10 x x x x   ♡ x x   ◊ A x x x   ♣ x x

This hand counts only 6 dummy points, but we would respond with a bid of 2 Spades. At least such action should serve as a partial pre-empt against fourth hand and in some cases may make it difficult for him to enter the auction.

However, let me point to an old slogan of mine: Don't let a fifth trump in dummy get you all excited.

Where dummy contains six trumps we have a freak situation, and delicacy of measurement cannot be achieved. In such cases your own instincts will generally serve as a reliable guide. In many cases a pre-emptive raise will be the best strategy despite a lack of point count. To point an extreme illustration, you are not vulnerable and your opponents are. Partner opens with 1 Spade. You hold:

♠ 10 x x x x x   ♡ x   ◊ Q x x   ♣ x x x

Unless partner has a powerhouse, opponents likely have a game. Some players would take a deliberate loss by pre-empting to 4 Spades. Occasionally such action might prove effective.

Responding with Strong Hands

(1) *The Jump Raise* (1 Spade—3 Spades)

This bid is forcing to game. Responder must have a little better than adequate trump support—usually four to an honor. The hand must contain 13 to 16 points. If your hand possesses the necessary point count, but lacks four trumps, you must temporize by naming a new suit and then supporting partner next round.

Partner opens with 1 Spade. You hold:

(A)		(B)		(C)	
♠ A 10 x x	(4)	♠ K J x x	(4)	♠ K 10 x x	(4)†
♡ x	(3)*	♡ A J x x	(5)	♡ x x x	
◊ x x x x		◊ x x	(1)x	◊ A K x	(7)
♣ A Q x x	(6)	♣ A x x	(4)	♣ K J x	(4)
	13		14		15

* Note singleton in supporting hand is worth 3 points.
x Note doubleton in supporting hand is worth 1 point.
† Note King of trumps in supporting hand is promoted.

In each case respond 3 Spades. Hand (C) counts 15 points. Even with the 1 point deduction for the defect of the 4-3-3-3 distribution it is still worth 14 points and fully qualifies for a jump raise.

(2) *The Triple Raise* (1 Spade—4 Spades)

This bid describes a hand with a great deal of trump support (usually five), a singleton or a void, but *not more than 9 points in high cards*, e.g.,

Partner opens 1 Spade. You hold:

♠ A J x x x
♡ x x
◊ x
♣ K 10 x x x

Respond 4 Spades. This hand is worth 12 points (8 points in high cards, 3 for the singleton and 1 for the doubleton). It is not a complete "shut-out" bid. But partner must not expect to find more than 9 points in high cards.

(3) *The Jump Take-out in No Trump* (1 Spade—2 No Trump)

This bid is forcing to game. Responder must have a balanced hand, with protection in all unbid suits and a point count of 13 to 15. The partnership is, therefore, assured of the necessary 26 points.

Partner opens with 1 Heart. You hold:

(A)			(B)		
♠ K J x	(4)		♠ A Q x	(6)	
♡ x x	*		♡ x x x		
◊ A J x x	(5)		◊ A J x	(5)	
♣ K J x x	(4)		♣ K J x x	(4)	
	___			___	
	13			15	

Respond 2 No Trump in both cases.

The Jump Take-out to 3 No Trump

This is a specialized bid that should be reserved for hands of the 4-3-3-3 distribution. With protection in all three unbid suits and a point count of 16 to 18, bid 3 No Trump.

Partner opens with 1 Spade. You hold:

(A)			(B)		
♠ J x x x	(1)		♠ Q x x	(2)	
♡ A Q x	(6)		♡ A J x	(5)	
◊ A J x	(5)		◊ K Q 10 x	(5)	
♣ K Q x	(5)		♣ A K x	(7)	
	___			___	
	17			19	

(A) Respond 3 No Trump.

(B) This hand is too big for a 3 No Trump response. The proper call is a *jump shift* to 3 Diamonds. Unless partner has a very light opening this hand will produce a good play for a slam.

* Remember that distributional values are not counted in bidding No Trump.

The Jump Shift

This bid is absolutely forcing to game and strongly suggests slam possibilities. It should be made only when responder has a strong suit of his own or good support for partner's suit. Responder's point count should be about 19.*

* Occasionally a jump shift may be made with 18 points, provided those points can be characterized as fourteen carat points. To put it in another way: If you are seized with an irresistible urge to make a bid, allow yourself one point for that urge.

Partner opens 1 Heart. You hold:

	(A)			(B)	
♠	A K Q J x x	(10)	♠	x	(3)
♡	x	(2)	♡	K Q x x	(5)
◊	A Q x x	(6)	◊	A x x	(4)
♣	x x	(1)	♣	A K x x x	(7)
		19			19

With hand (A) a jump shift to 2 Spades is indicated. You have no support for partner, but have a self-sustaining suit of your own. Since Spades are the contemplated trump you should value the hand as though you were the bidder. It has the value of 19 points, 16 in high cards, 2 for the singleton and 1 for the doubleton.

With hand (B) make a jump shift to 3 Clubs. Since Hearts are the contemplated trumps you should value your hand as a dummy. This, too, is worth 19 points, 16 in high cards and 3 for the singleton.

Responder Shows a New Suit at
the Level of 2

This is a constructive bid and should be based on a fairly good hand. How good? Assuming your hand to be more or less evenly balanced you must not go into the 2 level with a new suit if your hand is an eligible 1 No Trump response. This is to say, if your *high card* values are no greater than 9 (exclusive of distribution), 1 No Trump is the proper response.

Where you have 10 points in high cards and a five card suit your hand is too good for 1 No Trump, and you must respond with a new suit, even if you must bid at the level of 2.

Partner opens 1 Spade. You hold:

(A)	(B)
♠ x x	♠ 10 x
♡ K x x	♡ x x x
◇ A 9 x x x	◇ A Q x x x
♣ Q x x	♣ K J 10

(C)	(D)
♠ x x	♠ x x
♡ x x x	♡ A x x
◇ A x	◇ x x
♣ A J 10 x x x	♣ K J x x x x

(A) Respond 1 No Trump. You have 9 points in high cards, which makes it eligible for 1 No Trump. Therefore, the hand is not considered strong enough for 2 Diamonds.

(B) Respond 2 Diamonds. Your hand contains 10 points in high cards, to which is added 1 point for distribution, bringing it up to 11 points. Any hand containing a five card suit plus 10 high card points is too strong for 1 No Trump.

(C) Respond 2 Clubs. This hand contains only 9 points in high cards, but it has two distributional points, bringing the total to 11. Too big for 1 No Trump. But proceed slowly afterwards.

(D) Respond 1 No Trump, despite the six card Club suit. This hand has only 8 points in high cards and is worth only 10 points in all.

1 No Trump Response
to a 1 Club Opening

(This is a specialized bid and should not be employed except in trained partnerships.)

Since a response of 1 No Trump normally shows a maximum of 9 points, and a 2 No Trump response a minimum of 13 points, when holding an in-between hand (containing 10, 11 or 12 points) responder must bid in a roundabout way, arranging to speak twice. The practice with these hands is frequently to bid a suit at the level of 2 (even if a suit must be manufactured for the purpose), and await partner's rebid before deciding on the second response.

However, when the opening bid is 1 Club, responder cannot very well respond with a new suit at the level of 2, since that would be a jump. Accordingly, many players have adopted the practice of using a 1 No Trump response to an opening Club bid in an exceptional manner. The 1 No Trump response to a Club bid denotes a hand possessing the following characteristics:

(1) A high card count of 10 or 11 points (a little short of a 2 No Trump response), sometimes shaded to 9 good points.

(2) An evenly balanced hand

(3) Potential stoppers in the other three suits

(4) No biddable major suit

A 1 No Trump response to a Club bid might, for example, be made on the following hand:

$$\spadesuit \ \text{K x x} \qquad (3)$$
$$\heartsuit \ \text{Q x x} \qquad (2)$$
$$\diamondsuit \ \text{A 10 x x} \qquad (4)$$
$$\clubsuit \ \text{J x x} \qquad (1)$$

Opener should not pass this response if he has somewhat more than a minimum. If he has 15 points, or occasionally even 14 points, he should rebid to 2 No Trump. If he has 16 points he may rely on responder for 10, and is in a position to bid 3 No Trump himself. It should be observed that this method of bidding does not embarrass responder when he holds less than 10 points opposite an opening Club bid. He may make a one over one response in any other suit or raise the Club suit. When this choice is presented, these players will frequently make a 1 Diamond response on a three card suit, permitting opener to bid again at the level of 1.

Responding with Adequate Trump Support

On hands containing adequate trump support for partner's major suit and a count of 7 to 10 points, it is sound policy to give partner a single raise in his suit in preference to showing your own suit. The reason is this:

Such hands are worth only one "forward going" bid. You cannot afford, with hands of this limited strength, to bid your own suit and also raise partner. The more important of the two choices (the raise of partner's major suit) should be selected.

Partner opens with 1 Heart. Next hand passes. You hold:

(A)		(B)		(C)	
♠ x	(3)	♠ x x x		♠ x x x	
♡ A x x x	(4)	♡ A J x	(5)	♡ A J x	(5)
◇ Q x x x	(2)	◇ x x	(1)	◇ x x	(1)
♣ K 10 x x	(3)	♣ K J x x x	(4)	♣ K Q x x x	(5)
	12		10		11

(A) This hand is worth 12 points in support of Hearts. It is therefore, not quite strong enough for a jump to 3 Hearts, which would be forcing to game. However, it is too strong for a single raise, the top limit of which is 10; so you should arrange to bid twice. This you may accomplish by a temporizing bid of 2 Clubs. If partner rebids 2 Hearts, you raise to 3, showing 11 or 12 points.

(B) This hand appears to have the value of 10 points; but 1 point must be deducted for a holding of only three trumps, giving it a true value of 9. The hand is, therefore, worth only one forward bid and the proper call is 2 Hearts, not 2 Clubs.

(C) This hand is 1 point stronger than hand (B). Its true value is 10 points. This places it on the borderline between hands worth a single raise and those worth two bids. (A judgment point.) You may exercise your own judgment. My own preference would be in favor of aggressive action in this case; and I would arrange to bid twice by first calling 2 Clubs. The reason for the optimism is that all my values are clear cut. If one of my points were, let us say, the Jack of Spades or the Jack of Diamonds, I would feel less bullish and would exercise my judgment on the conservative side. I would in that case, respond merely 2 Hearts.

Responding After a Previous Pass

When a player has previously passed he must adopt a somewhat different attitude towards his responses. He must bear in mind that those responses are now no longer forcing (except a jump in a new suit). The mere naming of a new suit does not force his partner to speak again, nor does a jump raise, nor a jump in No Trump.

Responder must therefore be prepared to play the hand at whatever bid he happens to make. There is no longer available to him the temporizing bid. It follows, too, that since his bids are not forcing and since for all practical purposes he has denied possession of 13 points by his original pass, he may now jump with less than the normally required 13 points.

The jump response of 2 No Trump may now be made with 11 or 12 points instead of 13.

Similarly responder may raise from 1 Spade to 3 Spades with a little less than the required 13, e.g., as South you hold:

♠ K x x x
♡ K x x
♢ x x
♣ A x x x

The bidding has proceeded:

South	West	North	East
Pass	Pass	1 Spade	Pass
?			

What do you bid now?

If you had not previously passed, a temporizing bid would be in order. For this hand is too good for a single raise (its value is above 10 points) and not good enough for a forcing jump raise (its value is less than 13 points). The value of this hand for the purpose of raising Spades is 12 points, 4 for the King of Spades (promoted), 3 for the King of Hearts, 1 for the doubleton, and 4 for the Ace of Clubs.

If you had not previously passed, you would have arranged to make two bids. First a temporizing bid of 2 Clubs (forcing for one round) and then a raise of Spades on the next round.

Now you are at perfect liberty to respond 3 Spades. Partner will not expect you to have 13 points since you have already passed. If he has a shaded third hand opening he need not go on.

It would be improper for you to respond 2 Clubs, for partner might pass. Occasionally you will hold a passed hand which contains 13 points (or even more when valued in support of partner). In such cases you may raise directly to 4 Hearts or 4 Spades.

Similarly, as South you hold:

♠ x x
♡ K J x
◊ A J x x
♣ K x x x

The bidding has proceeded:

South	West	North	East
Pass	Pass	1 Spade	Pass
?			

What do you bid now?

If you had not previously passed you would temporize by bidding 2 Diamonds, a one round force. The hand is too strong for a 1 No Trump response (it has more than 10 points in high cards) and it is too weak for a game forcing response of 2 No Trump (it has less than 13 points in high cards).

Now, having 12 points, you may respond with 2 No Trump which is no longer forcing. If partner does not have more than 13 he need not go on.

Similarly a two over one response may be made with a little less after a previous pass.

As South you hold:

♠ x x
♡ x x x
◊ K x x
♣ A Q 10 x x

The bidding has proceeded:

South	West	North	East
Pass	Pass	1 Spade	Pass
?			

What do you bid now?

If you had not previously passed it would be improper to respond 2 Clubs. Your hand would not be good enough to force partner to rebid at the level of 2. The proper response would have been 1 No Trump. (The hand contains only 9 points in high cards.) But now you may respond 2 Clubs because your bid is not forcing and partner need not go on. 2 Clubs may prove to be the best place to play for a part score.

Jump Shift After Previous Pass

A jump shift in normal sequences is, of course, forcing to game and is suggestive of slam. But after a previous pass, a JUMP SHIFT IS ABSOLUTELY FORCING FOR ONE ROUND.

Suppose, as dealer, you have chosen to pass the following hand:

♠ K x x x x x   ♡ x   ◇ A Q J x   ♣ x x

and partner opens with 1 Spade. You dare not bid 3 Spades, for partner might pass. Even 4 Spades would not do justice to your holding, for it is unlikely that partner will be in position to take further action and a slam might easily be missed. The proper call is a jump shift of 3 Diamonds. Partner must speak once more, and Spades are supported on the next round. In no other way is it possible to overcome the effect of your previous pass.

CHAPTER X

FREE BIDS

ALL FREE BIDS must be based upon fairly good hands. When your right hand opponent has entered the auction, your partner automatically receives another chance to bid. It is, therefore, not necessary for you to strain a point to keep the bidding open with doubtful holdings.

Free Bid of 1 No Trump

A free bid of 1 No Trump describes a hand that is just a little better than an ordinary negative 1 No Trump response (the top limit of which is 10), but not quite as good as a 2 No Trump response (the lower limit of which is 13). In other words, a free bid of 1 No Trump usually describes a hand with 10 or 11 points, sometimes shaded as low as 9.

As South you hold:

(A)	(B)
♠ K 10 x	♠ K 10 x
♡ x x x	♡ x x x
◊ A x x	◊ A Q x
♣ J x x x	♣ J x x x

The bidding has proceeded:

North	East	South
1 Heart	1 Spade	?

With (A) you should pass. Do not bid 1 No Trump merely for the purpose of showing the Spade stopper. You have only 8 points. If East had passed you would, of course, be expected to respond with 1 No Trump.

With (B) you should call 1 No Trump. You have 10 points and a stopper in the adverse suit.

The Single Raise As a Free Bid

A raise for the purpose of keeping the bidding open may be made with as little as 7 points. But when your right hand opponent inserts a bid, you should not make a free raise with less than 9 points (7 and 8 represent a weak raise; 9 and 10 represent a good raise). On the other hand, a free single raise may be made with as many as 12 points (just a shade below a double raise).

As South you hold:

(A)	(B)
♠ x x	♠ x x
♡ K x x x	♡ Q x x x
◇ x x x	◇ x x x
♣ A x x x	♣ K x x x

The bidding has proceeded:

North	East	South
1 Heart	1 Spade	?

With (A) bid 2 Hearts; your hand has the value of 9 points —4 for the King of Hearts (promoted), 4 for the Ace, and 1 for the doubleton.

With (B) pass. You would have raised to 2 Hearts had East passed. But this hand is not good enough for a free raise inasmuch as it counts but 7 points.

The One Over One As a Free Bid

Even at the level of 1 a free bid should denote a fairly good hand and therefore should not be made with less than 9 or 10 points.

When your free bid of a new suit must be made at the level of 2, slightly more strength will be expected of you.

As South you hold:

	(A)			(B)	
♠	A x x	(4)	♠	x x x x	
♡	K J x x x	(4)	♡	K Q x x	(5)
◇	x x	(1)	◇	x x	(1)
♣	x x x		♣	A x x	(4)
		9			10

The bidding has proceeded:

North	East	South
1 Club	1 Diamond	?

In both cases you may make a free bid of 1 Heart. In (A) you have 9 points, in (B) 10 points.

But if you hold:

♠	x x	(1)
♡	x x x	
◇	A K J x x	(8)
♣	x x x	
		9

And the bidding has proceeded:

North	East	South
1 Spade	2 Clubs	?

You should not make a free bid of 2 Diamonds. A free bid of a new suit at the level of 2 requires about 11 points.

But if your free bid at the level of 2 must be made in a suit that is higher in rank than your partner's, so that the bidding will naturally be jammed up to a high level, you will need about 12 or 13 points, about the equivalent of an opening bid. The same requirements apply if your first response must be made at the level of 3.

As South you hold:

♠ A K x x x (7)
♡ Q x x   (2)
◇ x x   (1)
♣ x x x

——
10

The bidding has proceeded:

North	East	South
1 Diamond	2 Clubs	?

Do not bid 2 Spades. This hand has the value of 10 points and is not strong enough to project the bidding to the level of 3, which a free bid of 2 Spades would do.

Change the holding slightly:

♠ x x x
♡ A K x x x
◇ Q J x
♣ x x

The bidding has proceeded:

North	East	South
1 Spade	2 Clubs	?

You may bid 2 Hearts with 11 points, for the bidding will not be forced into the 3 level by such action.

CHAPTER XI

RESPONSES TO 2 BIDS

THE METHOD I employ myself, and which I heartily recommend to you, is the simplest, the soundest, and the one that has proven the most effective throughout the years. It is not spectacular; it is not dramatic; but it is natural and logical and imposes no additional burden on what by now may be your overtaxed memory.

The negative response remains, as always, 2 No Trump. But where specific values are held the practice is this:

FIRST MAKE A NATURAL RESPONSE. THEN, WHEN THE TRUMP SUIT HAS BEEN ESTABLISHED, THE PARTNERSHIP SHOWS EACH ACE AND EACH KING INDIVIDUALLY.

The natural response may take the form of a simple raise (the most preferable response when adequate trump support is held) or a simple suit take-out, or a response of 3 No Trump. The minimum requirement in each case is 7 points, including one quick trick, or 8 points including one-half a quick trick.

Don't lose sight of the fact that responder may have:

(a) trump support, or
(b) a good suit of his own, or
(c) Aces and Kings.

All three factors are of vital importance, and perhaps they rank in the order I have stated them. In a pinch good card reading may permit you to make a fairly good stab at whether your partner has a certain Ace or King, but you can hardly be expected to guess that your partner has trump support for you, or that he has a good five card suit.

Let us examine a few illustrations.

Opener	Responder
♠ A K x	♠ Q J 10 x x
♡ A K Q J 10 x	♡ x x x
◇ A x	◇ x x
♣ x x	♣ A x x

The bidding:

Opener	Responder
2 Hearts	2 Spades (1)
3 Hearts (2)	4 Clubs (3)
7 Hearts or	
7 No Trump (4)	

(1) In partnership language, "I have a hand containing at least 7 points including one quick trick and a five card suit headed by at least the Q-J."

(2) "The Heart suit is self-sustaining and you may consider that I have fixed it as the established trump. Start showing your Aces."

(3) "I have the Ace of Clubs."

(4) "That's all I wanted to know. I can count thirteen tricks because I know you have a five card Spade suit and we have six Hearts, five Spades and two Aces. I was glad to hear about your Spade suit, for the Ace of Clubs alone would bring the total of tricks only up to ten."

Another example:

Opener	Responder
♠ A K Q x x	♠ J 9 x x
♡ K Q J x	♡ A x x
◇ A Q J x	◇ K x
♣ None	♣ x x x x

The bidding:

Opener	Responder
2 Spades	3 Spades (1)
4 Diamonds (2)	4 Hearts (3)
5 Hearts (4)	6 Diamonds (5)
7 Spades (6)	

(1) "I have trump support for you, at least 7 points with one quick trick, and shall tell you about Aces on the next round."

(2) "I have the Ace of Diamonds. Keep talking."

(3) "I have the Ace of Hearts, in case you are interested."

(4) "Charmed! I have the King of Hearts. What else have you to tell me?"

(5) "I'm sure you're interested in the King of Diamonds."

(6) "It's a pleasure to do business with you. Some fellows would have had the Ace of Clubs instead of the Ace of Hearts, or the King of Clubs instead of the King of Diamonds. I'm spreading this hand for a grand slam and hope that the 'sucker' on my left, with the Ace of Clubs, decides to double me."

Another example:

Opener	Responder
♠ A K	♠ x x
♡ A K 10 x x x x	♡ Q 9 x
◇ A x	◇ K x x x
♣ x x	♣ A x x x

The bidding:

Opener	Responder
2 Hearts	3 Hearts (1)
3 Spades (2)	4 Clubs (3)
4 Diamonds (4)	5 Diamonds (5)
6 No Trump (6)	

(1) "Normal trump support with at least 7 points including one quick trick. Start the description."

(2) "I have the Ace of Spades."

(3) "I have the Ace of Clubs."

(4) "I have the Ace of Diamonds."

(5) "I have the King of Diamonds."

(6) "I can count twelve top card tricks on the basis of the three things you have told me. (The one I appreciate the most was the Heart support)."

Incidentally at this point opener could temporize still further by bidding 5 Spades, showing the King. This would afford responder the chance to bid 6 Clubs if he had the King of Clubs, or conceivably 6 Diamonds if he had the Queen.

It will be observed that the first mention of a suit, after trump has been fixed, shows the Ace. After the Ace has been shown, the next mention of that suit shows the King. After the Ace and King of a suit have been shown there will rarely be room for any further conversation, but if there should chance to be there is no reason why the third mention of the suit should not designate the Queen.

Ace Showing Over 2 Bids

"Do you show Aces over 2 bids?" is a question you will be confronted with on many occasions. Some players, in response to an opening 2 bid, make it a practice to show Aces and Kings wholesale and without regard to the rest of the hand. They proceed upon the theory that the opening bidder's first named suit will be the final trump and that the suit is self-sustaining. This is an entirely improper assumption. Their convention is a flashback to the old Sims' 3 Bid, which in those days was used to designate a hand of the same strength as an opening 2 bid, except that the trump suit was absolutely solid and the only thing opening bidder lacked was

Aces. It was a convention devised for freak hands; and it is not soundly applicable to our type of 2 demand bid, which may be based on a two suiter, or a suit that requires some support.

I believe in freedom of movement. I do not choose to have myself restricted to the showing of Aces and Kings only, when for no extra fee I may tell my partner whether I have support for his trumps or a suit of my own. Then I can show all the Aces and Kings I'm fortunate enough to hold, on later rounds.

In a word, when there is a choice between a natural and an artificial method, you are safe in wagering that over the course of time the natural method will prove superior.

I'm old-fashioned enough to be interested in whether my partner has trump support for me. Many a 2 bid lacks the Queen of trumps. It's comforting to learn that partner has it.

Take the hand of pages 23-24:

♠ A K J x x
♡ A
◇ A K x
♣ K Q 10 x

You open with 2 Spades. If partner holds hand (A) below a splendid play for slam is offered, despite the fact that it is Aceless. So responder, whose hand is worth 9 points in support of Spades, gives an immediate raise. Whereas hand (B), containing an Ace, presents virtually no play for slam.

(A)	(B)
♠ Q x x x	♠ x x
♡ K x x x x	♡ x x x x
◇ x x x	◇ x x x x
♣ x	♣ A x x

—— *IN BRIEF* ——

In making No Trump responses only the high card values are counted.

—————

In making suit responses you may add the distributional points to your high card values.

—————

In raising partner's suit bid you must employ the table of valuation for dummy hand, as follows:
  (A) Count high cards at face value
  (B) Promote honors in partner's suit
  (C) Add 1 point for a doubleton
      3 points for a singleton
      5 points for a void
Deduct 1 point if your hand contains only three trumps.
Deduct 1 point if your hand is distributed 4-3-3-3.

—————

Respond 1 No Trump   6-10 points
Respond 2 No Trump   13-15 points
Respond 3 No Trump   16-18 points

—————

Raise partner's suit bid to 2   7-10 points
Raise partner's suit bid to 3   13-16 points
Make a jump shift   19 points

—————

Show a new suit at 1 level   6 points
Show a new suit at 2 level   10 points

With hands counting 11 or 12 points find two bids forcing partner to game.

CHAPTER XII

REBIDS BY OPENER

Judging the Strength of My Hand As Opener

POINT COUNT

(13 to 16)

MY HAND IS IN THE MINIMUM RANGE. *If I don't feel like it I shall not bid again unless my partner's response is forcing. If he gives me a single raise I shall pass. If he responds with 1 No Trump I shall pass unless my hand is unbalanced. If he names a new suit I shall be obliged to bid again, but I shall rebid at the most convenient level. My rebid will be 1 No Trump, or a repetition of my original suit, or some other suit that I can show cheaply. Or I may have to give partner a single raise.*

(16 to 19)

I HAVE A GOOD HAND *and I am in a position to make a constructive rebid. I shall avoid making any rebid which my partner may construe as discouraging.*

(19 to 21)

I HAVE A VERY GOOD HAND. *This is in the jump rebid range. I will either jump in No Trump, or jump in my own suit or in partner's suit. Unless something was wrong with partner's response, we will surely have game.*

(22 and up)

THIS IS A SUPER HAND. *Of course, we are going*

to game. I'll personally see to that by making a jump shift, which partner is not permitted to pass and which is forcing to game. If partner has a good hand we will have a slam.

WHEN RESPONDER raises the opening bid from 1 to 2, opener must revalue his hand. In making his original bid the opening bidder counted his high cards, together with his distributional values. He added 1 point for a doubleton and 2 points for a singleton and 3 points for a void. That was another way of saying that the fifth card of the trump suit was valued at 1 point, and so was the sixth card. In other words a suit like this: A K x x x—was valued at 8 points; and this: A K x x x x—was valued at 9 points.

That was a reasonable enough valuation at the time he picked his hand up, and before he knew that a fit would be established. But when partner raises, his hand undergoes a transformation. That doubtful five or six card suit now becomes solidified and the long cards are worth considerably more than they were before. This adjustment is made in the following manner:

WHEN PARTNER RAISES YOUR SUIT, ADD AN ADDITIONAL POINT FOR THE FIFTH TRUMP AND 2 ADDITIONAL POINTS FOR THE SIXTH, AND EACH SUBSEQUENT TRUMP.

I'm sorry to have to burden your memory with this one, but it's indispensable if you want to value your hand properly. If this adjustment is not made, here is what you are apt to be confronted with: you open 1 Spade and partner raises to 2; you hold:

♠ A K J x x x
♡ A Q x
♢ x x x
♣ x

This hand has an original valuation of 16 points (14 in high cards and 2 for distribution). Since partner's raise may be based on as little as 7 points, you might not feel warranted in contracting for game. However you test him out by bidding only 3 and coaxing him to go forward. The poor unfortunate character, however, has raised on this colorless holding:

♠ x x x x
♡ J x
♦ K Q x x
♣ x x x

He has just 7 points, and quickly drops you at the 3 level. Here you are—playing for part score, though you are an outstanding favorite to go game.

What's wrong? You didn't revalue your hand after the raise. Add another point for the fifth trump and 2 points for the sixth, and your real valuation is now 19. Since partner has promised 7 points there's nothing more to wait for. You utter the words "Four Spades," and proceed with the relatively easy business of fulfilling your contract.

We apologize for adding this to the long string of figures you must commit to memory, but there is this bit of news that will be relished by the tired businessman: We have no more tables of values to offer you.

Raising Responder from 1 to 2
(14-15-16 POINTS)

Where opener has support for responder's major suit, he may raise from 1 to 2 with very little more *than a minimum* opening. Opener now revalues his hand as though it were a dummy for his partner; and if he has a little more than 13, which is the normal minimum opening, he may raise. A raise should not be made with less than 14 (1 point over the minimum), except when four trumps are held.

You open 1 Club. Partner responds 1 Spade. You hold:

(A) ♠ A x x   ♡ x   ◇ x x x x   ♣ A K J x x (14)*
(B) ♠ A x x x   ♡ x x   ◇ J 10 x   ♣ A K J x   (14)*
(C) ♠ A x x   ♡ x x   ◇ x x x   ♣ A K J x x (13)*

With hands (A) and (B) raise to 2 Spades. They each have 14 points (a little over minimum) with trump support for partner. With hand (C) rebid 2 Clubs. This is an absolute minimum, and the raise should not be given.

Raising Responder from 1 to 3
(17 TO 19 POINTS)

You open 1 Club. Partner responds 1 Spade. You hold:

♠ A x x x (4)
♡ K Q x x (5)
◇ x   (3)
♣ A Q x x (6)

Bid 3 Spades. Your hand has a value of 18 points in support of Spades.

You open 1 Diamond. Partner responds 1 Spade. You hold:

♠ A x x x   (4)
♡ K x   (4)
            (3 for King; 1 for doubleton)
◇ A K J x x (8)
♣ x x   (1)

Bid 3 Spades. Your hand has a value of 17 points in support of Spades. This bid is not forcing. Responder may exercise his option to pass if his response was based on 6 or 7 points. However, if his response contained 8 or 9 points, he must go on.

*These hands are all revalued as in support of a Spade bid by partner.

Raising Responder from 1 to 4
(AT LEAST 20 POINTS)

You open 1 Club. Partner responds 1 Spade. You hold:

♠ K Q x x   (5)
♡ A J x x   (5)
◇ x   (3)
♣ A K J x   (8)

Bid 4 Spades. Your hand has the value of 21 points in support of Spades. This bid is by no means a shut out; and if partner has 11 or 12 points he should show some animation. Let us have none of this Gay Nineties chatter—"Partner, you jumped to game, that shut me out!"

Where the opener's hand is worth 22 points in support of partner, serious consideration should be given to a jump shift rebid.

Jump Rebid to 2 No Trump
(19 AND 20 POINTS)

♠ x x
♡ K Q x   (5)
◇ A K J x   (8)
♣ A Q x x   (6)

You open 1 Diamond. Partner responds 1 Spade. You have 19 points in high cards. It will take about 7 in partner's hand to reach the required 26; but he may not have that many. He may have as little as 5 in high cards (plus perhaps another point for distribution). You are therefore not in position to contract for game. You should jump to 2 No Trump. If partner has 7 he must go on to game. Even if he has only 6 points in high cards, he'll probably take a chance.

Jump Rebid to 3 No Trump
(21 AND 22 POINTS)

- ♠ 10 x
- ♡ A Q x   (6)
- ◊ A K J x (8)
- ♣ A Q J x (7)

You open 1 Diamond. Partner responds 1 Spade. You have 21 points in high cards. Even if partner has a shaded response you will have the required 26. Bid 3 No Trump.

Jump Rebid in Opener's Own Suit
(16 TO 19 POINTS)

You open 1 Heart and partner responds 1 Spade. You are contemplating a bid of 3 Hearts. This may be done with 16 or 17 points provided opener has a solid five card suit or a very good six card suit.

- ♠ x x   (1)
- ♡ A K 10 x x x (7)
- ◊ A Q x   (6)
- ♣ K x   (4)

(3 for King; 1 for doubleton)

Rebid 3 Hearts. Your hand is worth 18 points and contains a good six card suit.

Jump Shift by Opener
(22 POINTS AND UP)

You open 1 Club. Partner responds 1 Spade. You hold:

- ♠ K x x x   (4)
- ♡ x   (3)
- ◊ A K x   (7)
- ♣ A K Q x x (9)

Bid 3 Diamonds. (A manufactured jump shift.) Your hand
is worth 23 points in support of Spades and is too big for a
raise to 4 Spades. The immediate slam signal should be
flashed.

Rebid by Opener When Responder Bids 2 of a New Suit

Whenever opening bidder on his rebid makes it impossible for responder to return to 2 of the first suit, he announces
a strong hand (somewhere between 16 and 19 points), e.g.,

	Opener	Responder
(a)	1 Heart	2 Diamonds
	2 No Trump	?
(b)	1 Heart	2 Diamonds
	3 Diamonds	?
(c)	1 Heart	2 Diamonds
	3 Clubs	?
(d)	1 Heart	2 Diamonds
	2 Spades	?
(e)	1 Spade	2 Hearts
	3 Hearts	

In each of these cases responder finds it impossible to return to 2 Hearts. Opener has therefore promised a strong
hand:

- (a) 15 to 18 points in high cards
- (b) 16 to 18 points in support
- (c) at least 17 rebid points
- (d) about 19 rebid points
- (e) this raise may be given with 15 points, or even
  a point less, where four of partner's trumps are
  held. In this respect it differs from a raise to 3
  of a minor suit which requires 16 points.

Examples of Rebids by Opener

You are South in the following hands. The bidding has proceeded:

South	North
1 Spade	1 No Trump
?	

What do you bid now?

(A)		(B)	
♠ A Q J 10 x	(7)	♠ A K x x	(7)
♡ Q J x	(3)	♡ A Q J x	(7)
◊ x x		◊ x x x	
♣ K x x	(3)	♣ x x	

(C)		(D)	
♠ A Q x x x	(6)	♠ A K J 10 x	(8)
♡ x x		♡ K J x	(4)
◊ A K x	(7)	◊ A x	(4)
♣ K Q x	(5)	♣ K Q x	(5)

(A) Pass. You have only 13 points in high cards. Even if partner has the maximum of 10, you will have no game. Your hand is balanced, and Spades should not be rebid.

(B) Bid 2 Hearts. With 4 Spades and 4 Hearts, strain, even with more or less minimum hands, to rebid 2 Hearts to guard against the situation in which partner had a Heart suit that he could not mention at the level of 2.

(C) Bid 2 No Trump, which in this sequence requires 18 or 19 points. If partner's No Trump is on the lower side (6 points) there will be no game and he will pass but if it is on the upper side (8 or 9 points) he should go on to 3 No Trump. With 7 points he may exercise his own judgment.

(D) Bid 3 No Trump. You have 21 points in high cards. Even if Partner has a minimum No Trump of only 6 points you will have enough.

You are South in the following hands. The bidding has proceeded:

	South	North
	1 Spade	2 Spades
	?	

What do you bid now?

(A)
♠ A K x x x	(7)
♡ A x x	(4)
◇ Q x x	(2)
♣ x x	(1)

(B)
♠ A K x x x	(7)
♡ A x x	(4)
◇ K J x	(4)
♣ x x	(1)

(C)
♠ A K x x	(7)
♡ A Q 10 x	(6)
◇ x x	(1)
♣ A x x	(4)

(A) Pass. Your hand has an original valuation of 14 points. Adding a point for the fifth card of your supported trump suit brings it up to 15 points. Even if partner has the maximum of 10, you will be slightly short of game.

(B) Bid 3 Spades. Your hand has an original valuation of 16 points. Adding a point for the fifth card of your supported trump suit brings the value to 17. If partner's raise was on the lower side (7 or 8 points) you will not have quite enough and he should pass, but if it is on the upper side (9 or 10 points) he should go on to 4 Spades.

(C) Bid 3 Hearts. Your hand has a value of 18 points. If partner's raise was based on 7 points there will probably be no game, but if it is based on a little more there will be. The 3 Heart bid asks him to go to game if his

raise was in the upper bracket. He must then bid either
4 Spades, 4 Hearts or 3 No Trump. If he returns to 3
Spades it will mean that he had a light raise and you
probably should quit.

———

As South you hold:

♠ A K x x x (7)
♥ x x   (1)
♦ K J x   (4)
♣ A x x   (4)

The bidding has proceeded:

South	North
1 Spade	3 Spades
?	

Your hand had an original valuation of 16 points. Adding
a point for the fifth card of your supported trump suit, your
hand is worth 17 points. North's hand ranges from 13 to 16
points. If it is maximum you may have a slam. Suggest it by
bidding 4 Clubs, showing the Ace. If partner merely returns
to 4 Spades, you will have done your duty and should retire.
If partner bids 4 Diamonds—you may carry on by bidding 5
Diamonds, showing the King. The rest will be up to him.

———

As South you hold:

♠ A K x x x (7)
♥ x x   (1)
♦ A Q x   (6)
♣ K Q x   (5)

The bidding has proceeded:

South	North
1 Spade	3 Spades
?	

Your hand had an original valuation of 19. Adding a point for the fifth card of your supported trump suit, your hand is worth 20 points. So, even if partner has a minimum of 13, you will have enough for a slam; and you may sit right up in your chair and bid 6 Spades, or you may get a little more mileage out of this hand by first bidding 4 Diamonds.

A word about forcing bids by opener. It has been said that a jump rebid by opener in his own suit is highly invitational, but not forcing. This is only a part truth. In the bidding sequence:

Opener	Responder
1 Heart	1 Spade
3 Hearts	

the 3 Heart bid is not forcing. Responder may pass with a minimum response.

But if responder has bid at an increased level, the jump rebid by opener is absolutely forcing. For example:

Opener	Responder
1 Heart	2 Clubs
3 Hearts	

The 3 Heart bid in this sequence is absolutely forcing to game because responder has shown upwards of 10 points.

Another forcing situation develops when opener names a new suit at the level of 3. For example:

Opener	Responder
1 Spade	2 Diamonds
3 Clubs	

The 3 Club bid is completely forcing. To put it in a phrase: When both partners are engaged in showing considerable strength, all bids are forcing.

CHAPTER XIII

REBIDS BY RESPONDER

Judging the Strength of My Hand As Responder

POINT COUNT

(6 to 10)

> *MY HAND IS IN THE MINIMUM RANGE AND I SHALL MAKE A MILD RESPONSE. However, I may act again if partner coaxes me to. If I have only 6 points I won't be coaxed to take further action. But if I have 8 or 9 points, and partner invites me to speak again, I shall do so cheerfully. With 7 points I shall use my own judgment.*

(10 to 13)

> *I HAVE A GOOD HAND. It is worth two bids; and to be sure that I get two chances I shall make a response which opener is not permitted to pass. That is, I will temporarily bid a new suit.*

(13 to 16)

> *I HAVE A VERY GOOD HAND AND MUST SEE TO IT THAT WE REACH GAME; for I have an OPENING BID FACING AN OPEN- ING BID. That is to say, our partnership has at least 26 points. I shall, therefore, either make an immediate game forcing bid, or keep making bids which opener may not pass (new suits) until we reach a satisfactory game contract.*

(16 to 19)

> *I HAVE A VERY POWERFUL HAND. A mere game demand response would not be sufficient. I must show that I have more than an opening bid. I may do this by jumping to 3 No Trump (instead of 2 No Trump), or by bidding a suit and then making a big jump the next round.*

(19 and up)

> *THIS HAND WILL PRODUCE A SLAM UNLESS PARTNER HAS A MINIMUM. I must, therefore, give the immediate slam signal by jumping in a new suit. The Jump Shift.*

Examples of Rebids by Responder

You are South in the following hands. The bidding has proceeded:

North	South
1 Spade	1 No Trump
2 No Trump	?

What do you bid now?

(A)		(B)	
♠ x x		♠ x x	
♡ Q x x	(2)	♡ K x x x	(3)
◊ K J x x	(4)	◊ Q x x	(2)
♣ Q x x x	(2)	♣ Q x x x	(2)

(A) Bid 3 No Trump. Your response contained 8 points in high cards; it was therefore in the upper bracket (it might have been only 6 or 7) and you should accept partner's invitation to proceed.

(B) Pass. Your hand has only 7 points and is in the lower side of the No Trump response. You should decline the invitation.

You are South in the following hands. The bidding has proceeded:

North	South
1 Spade	2 Spades
3 Spades	?

What do you bid now?

(A)		(B)	
♠ Q x x x	(3)	♠ Q x x x	(3)
♡ x x	(1)	♡ x x	(1)
◊ Q x x x	(2)	◊ K x x x	(3)
♣ A x x	(4)	♣ x x x	

(A) Bid 4 Spades. Your hand is worth 10 points, which makes it a maximum raise. (Note the Queen of trumps is promoted to the value of a King.)

(B) Pass. Your hand is worth only 7 points, which places it in the lower bracket, and you should decline the invitation.

As South you hold:

♠ J x x	(1)
♡ A K x x	(7)
◊ K x x x	(3)
♣ x x	

The bidding has proceeded:

North	South
1 Club	1 Heart
1 No Trump	?

Don't give up the ship. You have 11 points in high cards and it is your duty to speak twice. Raise to 2 No Trump. Partner may have 15 points, in which case he will carry on.

As South you hold:

      ♠ x x x
      ♡ A 10 x x x (4)
      ◊ x x   (1)
      ♣ A x x   (4)

The bidding has proceeded:

North	South
1 Diamond	1 Heart
2 Diamonds	?

Pass. Your hand has the value of only 9 points (including the point for distribution) and you are entitled to only one bid. Partner cannot have as many as 17 points else he would have made an encouraging rebid.

As South you hold the following hands:

	(A)			(B)	
♠	x x		♠	x x	
♡	A K x x x	(7)	♡	A K x x x	(7)
◊	Q J x	(3)	◊	J x x	(1)
♣	K J x	(4)	♣	K J x	(4)

	(C)			(D)	
♠	J x x	(1)	♠	J x x	(1)
♡	A K x x x	(7)	♡	A K x x x	(7)
◊	x x	(1)	◊	x x	(1)
♣	K J x	(4)	♣	Q x x	(2)

The bidding has proceeded:

North	South
1 Spade	2 Hearts
2 Spades	?

(A) Your hand is well adapted to No Trump play and you have a high card point count of 14. Even if partner has a minimum you will have enough and your proper bid is 3 No Trump.

(B) Since partner has not supported Hearts and you cannot support Spades an effort should be made to reach a No Trump game. You cannot quite reach it yourself, for you have only 12 points and you have not complete protection in Diamonds, but you should move in that direction by bidding 2 No Trump, which partner will pass only if he has opened a minimum hand. If he has 14, he should go to 3.

(C) Bid 4 Spades. You have normal trump support for a rebid suit and your hand has the value of 13 points in support of Spades. (Remember the Jack of Spades is promoted but there is a deduction for only three trumps.) The partnership, therefore, presumably has 26 points.

(D) Bid 3 Spades. Your hand is worth only 11 points in support of Spades and partner must be given a chance to pass if he has a minimum. (Remember there is a deduction of 1 point for only three trumps.)

As South you hold:

♠ x x   (1)
♡ A K 10 x x (7) + 1 rebid point
◇ x x x
♣ Q x x   (2)

The bidding has proceeded:

North	South
1 Diamond	1 Heart
2 Hearts	?

Your hand had an original value of 10 points; adding 1 point for the fifth card of the supported Heart suit brings the total to 11. Partner's hand is known to range from 14 to 16. If it happens to be 15 or 16, you will have enough. You should, therefore, coax partner to go on by bidding 3 Hearts.

♠ x x   (1)
♡ A K 10 x x (7) + 1 rebid point
◇ x x x
♣ K J x   (4)

The bidding has proceeded as above. You should bid 4 Hearts.
Your hand has a rebid value of 13 points. Partner is known
to have at least 14.

As South you hold:

♠ x x x
♡ A J x x x   (5) + 1 rebid point
◇ K Q x   (5)
♣ x x   (1)

The bidding has proceeded:

North	South
1 Spade	2 Hearts
3 Hearts	?

You should bid 4 Hearts. Your hand has a rebid value of 12
points. Partner has at least 14 points. You therefore have
the necessary 26 points.

As South you hold:

♠ K Q 10 x   (5)
♡ K Q x x   (5)
◇ A x   (5)
♣ x x x

The bidding has proceeded:

North	South
1 Diamond	1 Spade
3 Spades	?

This hand has the value of 15 points. North has shown a
holding ranging from 17 to 19, placing you in the slam

zone. You should bid 4 Diamonds, showing the Ace and await your partner's reaction. This is a very probable slam.

As South you hold:

```
♠ x x        (1)
♡ A K J x x  (8)  + 1 rebid point
♢ K Q x      (5)
♣ J 10 x     (1)
```

The bidding has proceeded:

North	South
1 Spade	2 Hearts
4 Hearts	?

Slam is in the air. Your hand has a rebid value of 16 points. Partner has opened and jumped in your suit, which marks him with a strong hand, probably 17 points or more. This adds up to enough count for a slam. You may check for Aces. A 4 No Trump bid at this point is a clear cut Blackwood bid and would protect you against partner's holding some hand like this:

```
♠ A K Q x x
♡ Q 10 x x
♢ x
♣ K Q x
```

As South you hold:

```
♠ A K J x x
♡ J x
♢ x x x
♣ K Q x
```

The bidding has proceeded:

North	South
1 Heart	1 Spade
2 No Trump	?

You have enough to warrant contraction for slam. Partner has promised at least 19 points. You have a high card count of 14, accounting for the required 33. In addition you have the following bullish features: a good five card suit to work with—the Jack of Hearts may be quite valuable. Bid 6 No Trump.

As South you hold:

♠ K x x
♥ x x
♦ A K 10 x x
♣ x x x

The bidding has proceeded:

North	South
1 Spade	2 Diamonds
2 No Trump	?

What do you bid now?

Answer: 3 Spades. Since partner has announced a holding of at least 16 points you know that you have enough for game, but you should give partner the choice between 4 Spades and 3 No Trump. Your 3 Spade bid is forcing, for partner can recognize that your team has 26 points. He knows he has 16 and since you responded with 2 of a new suit, he knows you have at least 10.

CHAPTER XIV

OVERCALLS

IN MAKING overcalls (i.e., when an opponent has opened the bidding) too much reliance should not be placed on point count. The consideration of paramount importance is the texture of your trump suit. When you overcall at the level of 2, you should promise partner that you won't lose more than two tricks in the trump suit itself.

Opponent opens 1 Spade. You hold:

(A)		(B)	
♠ x x x		♠ x x	(1)
♡ A x	(5)	♡ K Q J 9 x x	(6)
◇ K x x	(3)	◇ A x x	(4)
♣ A Q x x x	(6)	♣ x x	(1)

Hand (A) is valued at 14 points (13 in high cards and 1 for doubleton). Hand (B) has the value of only 12 points (10 in high cards and 1 each for the doubletons). Yet hand (B) is a much better overcall, for you are in a position to promise that you will not lose more than two trump tricks if you overcall with 2 Hearts.

With hand (A) (call me a timid soul if you choose), I would not overcall with 2 Clubs. I could very easily lose three or four tricks in Clubs alone.

When I overcall, I like to make sure that if doubled I won't go down more than 500 points. There is nothing like 800 or 1100 sets to impair one's social standing. To overcall at the level of 2 one must be working with a good trump suit, or on a liberal cash allowance.

One of the prime inducements in making an overcall is to suggest a good lead to partner. That's why overcalls on Jack-high suits stand in such little favor.

Opponent opens 1 Diamond. You hold:

(A)		(B)	
♠ x x x		♠ x x x	
♡ J 9 x x x	(1)	♡ K Q J x x	(6)
◇ A x	(5)	◇ x x	(1)
♣ K J x	(4)	♣ K x x	(3)

Both hands are valued at 10 points. I would overcall 1 Heart with (B) but not with (A).

An overcall of 1 No Trump should be based on a hand that would have been a sound opening 1 No Trump bid (16 to 18 points), and the adverse suit must be safely stopped.

To summarize: To overcall at the level of 1 you should have at least 10 points. But the mere possession of 10 points does not justify an overcall.

To overcall at the level of 2 you should have at least 12 points and a very good suit.

The Pre-Emptive Jump Overcall

The pendulum of time has swung back a couple of decades and we have now reverted to the use of the jump overcall as a pre-emptive measure.

Many players refer to this practice as "the weak jump overcall," a term which is ill advised. For the overcall is weak only as regards high card content. The suit itself, however, should be reasonably good. The pre-emptive jump overcall is a more descriptive term than "weak jump overcall."

One of the advantages of the pre-emptive jump overcall is that it offers to partner a more or less accurate picture of the holding and frequently lays the groundwork for an eventual sacrifice bid if that should prove desirable.

Specifications for the single jump overcall are quite precise, and strict adherence to the requirements is recommended for greatest effectiveness. The bid should be based on a good suit at least six cards in length. The maximum high card strength is 9 points and most of these should be concentrated in the bid suit. The 2 and 3 trick principle of potential loss should be employed when considering this call, i.e., the bidder should be able to hold his losses to 500 points if he gets doubled.

Let us examine a few instances where you are South and the player on your right has opened the bidding with 1 Heart. Neither side is vulnerable.

(A)	(B)
♠ K J 10 9 x x x	♠ x x
♡ x x	♡ x
◇ Q x x	◇ x x x
♣ x	♣ K Q J 10 9 x x

(C)	(D)
♠ J 10 9 x x x x	♠ K x x x
♡ A	♡ x
◇ x x x	◇ Q J 10 9 x x x
♣ A x	♣ x

Hands (A) and (B) are excellent examples of the pre-emptive jump overcall. Observe that in the second hand where the single jump necessitates bidding at the 3 level, the bid is still considered to be pre-emptive in nature.

In the third and fourth hands a simple overcall is preferred. Hand (C) contains too much defensive strength for a pre-emptive bid and (D) has a reasonable holding in a secondary suit. A jump overcall should suggest a strictly one suited hand and a bid of 3 Diamonds might block your side out of a Spade contract if partner should fit that suit.

The Unusual No Trump Overall

One of the modern developments in Contract Bridge is the Unusual No Trump Overcall which provides that when the other side opens the bidding and a player makes an overcall in any number of No Trumps that could not possibly mean what it says, it is to be interpreted as a take-out double asking partner to respond in his best minor suit.

For example, you are South and hold:

♠ A x   ♡ x   ◇ K Q 10 x x   ♣ K Q 9 x x

The bidding has proceeded:

West	North	East	South
1 Spade	Pass	2 Spades	?

If you bid 3 Diamonds and get doubled, there will be considerable doubt in your mind whether to stay there or to try Clubs at a higher level. On the other hand, if you try a take-out double, partner is apt to respond in Hearts, a response with which you are ill prepared to cope. As a matter of fact, whenever you double one major suit there is a strong suggestion that you would like partner to respond in the other major. In the present instance, therefore, in order to elicit a choice from partner between the two minor suits, you bid 2 No Trump. This cannot, from a common sense viewpoint, be construed as a natural bid, and partner should bid either Diamonds or Clubs even if he has to make his call in a three card suit.

There are certain cases where an overcall in No Trump still means what it says. The most common instances occur where the overcall comes immediately after the opening bid. For example, you are South in each of the following hands and East has opened the bidding with 1 heart.

(A)	(B)
♠ A Q	♠ K x x
♡ K J x	♡ A Q
◊ A J 10 x x	◊ K Q J x x
♣ Q x x	♣ A Q J

(C)	(D)
♠ A x	♠ x
♡ K x	♡ x
◊ A K Q J x x	◊ K Q x x x x
♣ A Q x	♣ A Q 10 x x

With (A) you bid 1 No Trump, a natural bid showing a balanced hand, 16-19 points and good protection in Hearts.

With (B) you bid 2 No Trump, a natural bid showing a balanced hand, 22-24 points and good protection in Hearts.

With (C) you bid 3 No Trump, a natural bid showing a balanced hand and the ability to win 9 tricks. This bid usually indicates a point count of 25-27, but in this case your 23 points are buttressed by a solid, six card suit.

With (D) you have no choice but to bid 2 Diamonds. An overcall in No Trump when made immediately over an opening bid is a natural call. In the present instance you will have to show your suits individually which should prove to be no great inconvenience.

CHAPTER XV

THE TAKE-OUT DOUBLE

THOUGH THE subject is not at all complex, considerable difficulty seems to be experienced by many Bridge players in the handling of this weapon. A condition which, it seems to me, can be rectified by just a bit of study.

When an opponent opens the bidding, more than average strength can be announced in several ways. The most usual is the take-out double.

"Partner, don't be intimidated by the opening bidder. My hand is probably as good as his. At any rate, it will make a good dummy." That is the message the take-out double is intended to convey. In other words, a take-out double shows a hand that is at least as good as an opening bid. That is to say, it should contain at least 13 points.

Your right hand opponent opens with 1 Club. You hold:

(A)		(B)	
♠ A 10 x x	(4)	♠ A K J x x	(8)
♡ K 9 x x	(3)	♡ A 10 x x	(4)
◇ K J x x	(4)	◇ x x x	
♣ x	(3)*	♣ x	(3)*
	—		—
	14		15

Holding either of these hands you should double.

* We think it is a good policy when making a take-out double to value your hand as though it were dummy which, indeed, it is anticipated it will eventually become.

(C)		(D)	
♠ x x x		♠ x x x	
♡ A K x	(7)	♡ A K x	(7)
◇ A x x	(4)	◇ A Q x	(6)
♣ x x x x		♣ x x x x	

Your right hand opponent has opened the bidding with 1 Spade, what should you do?

In both cases you should pass.

Hand (C) contains but 11 points—hand (D) contains 13 points. But since these hands will have to be dummy for partner, it is sound policy to deduct a point from each for its flaw. They have the defect of possessing a 4-3-3-3 distribution as a prospective dummy. Proper application of the point count in this situation will actually safeguard the less experienced player against certain errors in judgment.

Possession of 13 or more points by the player contemplating a take-out double will usually, but not necessarily, protect against these errors in judgment. However, it must be borne in mind that the doubler, in addition to having the required point count, must promise partner that his hand will be a good dummy. Either that, or the doubler must have a reasonably safe contract in mind. In a word, the take-out doubler must promise safety. Observe the following case:

♠ A Q x x	(6)
♡ x	(2)
◇ A x x x	(4)
♣ A J x x	(5)
	—
	17

Your right hand opponent opened the bidding with 1 Spade. Despite the fact that your hand has a value of 17 points, it would not be a sound take-out double inasmuch as you must be prepared for partner's expected response of 2 Hearts. In that case your hand would not be a good dummy, and you have not the high card values to justify a bid of 2 No Trump, which would be your only out. There is nothing left for you to do, therefore, but to make a trap pass.

Had your right hand opponent opened with 1 Heart your hand would have been an ideal double. It would also have been acceptable for a take-out double if the adverse bid had been 1 Club or 1 Diamond; for, if partner made the expected response of 1 Heart, you would at least be in a position where you might escape with reasonable safety to 1 Spade.

Be careful of take-out doubles with evenly balanced hands. Remember you must subtract a point in that case if you hold a 4-3-3-3.

Be careful, too, about doubling when your principal strength is in the adverse suit.

Take-out Double of 1 No Trump

A take-out double should represent a hand that is presumably as strong as the opening bidder's. Therefore, when making an immediate double of 1 No Trump you should have at least 16 points in high cards. LEAVE IN AN IMMEDIATE DOUBLE OF 1 NO TRUMP IF YOU HAVE AT LEAST 6 POINTS IN HIGH CARDS. For example:

As South you hold:

♠ 10 x
♡ x x x
♢ Q x x   (2)
♣ K J x x x (4)

The bidding has proceeded:

West	North	East	South
1 No Trump	Double	Pass	?

You should pass. Here is the arithmetic: partner has at least 16, you have 6; the partnership, therefore, has at least 22 points, whereas the opponents have at most 18. Bear in mind that the opening bidder's dummy will have at most 2 points and perhaps less. Since you outnumber them in count, you will win more tricks than they and you should play for the penalty.

Take-out Double to Reopen the Bidding

This bid may be made with as little as 11 points. For example:

As South you hold:

♠ A x x x   (4)
♡ K x x x   (3)
◊ K J x   (4)
♣ x x   (1)
            ——
            12

The bidding has proceeded:

West	North	East	South
1 Club	Pass	Pass	?

With this hand you may double to reopen the bidding in order to permit your side to try for the part score. Doubler's partner should view the take-out double in this situation with some measure of suspicion, unless doubler confirms the soundness of his double by subsequent action.

CHAPTER XVI

RESPONSES TO THE TAKE-OUT DOUBLE

A NATURAL tendency of players is to undervalue their hands as responder to a take-out double. This table is recommended to assist you in forming an estimate of your holding.

A hand containing 6 points is a fair hand.
A hand containing 9 points is a good hand.
A hand containing 11 points is a probable game hand.
Partner doubles 1 Heart. You hold:

(A)		(B)	
♠ A J x x x	(5)	♠ A J x x x	(5)
♡ x x x		♡ x x x	
◇ x x x		◇ K x x	(3)
♣ x x	(1)	♣ x x	(1)
	—		—
	6		9

(C)		(D)	
♠ A J x x x	(5)	♠ A J x x x x	(5)
♡ x x x		♡ x x x	
◇ K Q x	(5)	◇ K J x	(4)
♣ x x	(1)	♣ x	(2)
	—		—
	11		11

(A) contains 6 points and is a fair hand.

(B) contains 9 points and is a good hand.

(C) and (D) contain 11 points each and, therefore, are probable game hands. You should respond with one more than is necessary, that is, 2 Spades.

The requirement for responding to partner's take-out double is *zero points*. The less you have, the more urgent it is to respond, else opponents will make their doubled contract with overtricks, which can prove very costly.

In responding to partner's take-out double prefer a four card major to a five card minor at the level of 1. For example:

♠ K x x x
♡ x x
♢ Q 10 x x x
♣ x x

Partner doubles 1 Heart. Respond 1 Spade rather than 2 Diamonds.

Your partner doubles 1 Diamond. You hold:

♠ K J x x   (4)
♡ A 10 x x   (4)
♢ x x x
♣ x x   (1)
              —
              9

Your hand has the value of 9 points. It is, therefore, a *good* hand. You should arrange to bid both suits in their logical order, showing Spades first.

In responding to a take-out double prefer a major suit to 1 No Trump, but prefer 1 No Trump to a minor suit if you hold a fairly good hand, that is, about 9 points in high cards. With only a single stopper in the suit bid by opponents it is perhaps more prudent to insist upon 10 points for a 1 No Trump response. For example, partner doubles a bid of 1 Heart, and you hold:

♠ x x
♡ Q J 9 x   (3)
♢ A 9 x   (4)
♣ Q 10 x x   (2)
——
9

Your best response is 1 No Trump. This hand contains 9 points, with a double Heart stopper. This is preferable to responding with 2 Clubs.

Your partner doubles 1 Heart. You hold:

♠ Q 9 x x   (2)
♡ K Q x   (5)
♢ Q x x   (2)
♣ x x x
——
9

While the hand has the strength to justify a 1 No Trump response to partner's double, that is, 9 points, a bid of 1 Spade is to be preferred.

If you have a fair hand you should bid again when partner jumps.

With a good hand you should bid again if partner takes any moderate action.

With 13 points, drastic action is mandatory. Make a bid which is absolutely forcing to game.

Even with 12 points, game will probably be reached and strong action is indicated.

Partner doubles 1 Club. You hold:

♠ K x x x   (3)
♡ A x x   (4)
♢ K Q x   (5)
♣ x x x
——
12

You have 12 points which should convince you that there is a game for your side and a jump response is indicated. Bid 2 Spades despite the weakness of the suit.

Your partner doubles 1 Club. You hold:

♠ K J x   (4)
♡ x x x
◇ Q J x x   (3)
♣ K Q x   (5)
                ——
                12

Holding 12 points you should make a jump response of 2 No Trump.

Notice this is a point less than is required for a 2 No Trump response to an opening suit bid. The reason is that your 2 No Trump bid in this sequence is not 100% forcing. If the take-out double has been shaded the doubler may take the liberty of passing.

Business Pass of Partner's Take-out Double

Don't pass partner's take-out double of 1 of a suit unless you are quite sure you will show a profit by doing so. Don't get panicky because you have a bad hand. When you speak in this position you are not making a bid in the true sense of the word. You are merely replying to partner's question, "What is your best suit, however weak it may be?" In order to justify passing his double you must have a reasonable expectancy of winning four tricks; and at least three of them should be in the trump suit.

This is not to be confused with a business pass of partner's immediate double of 1 No Trump. Such a double may be left in if you have 6 points.

Procedure by Doubler's Partner After an Intervening Bid

A free response should be made if doubler's partner holds a fairly good hand, that is, about 8 points, counting both high

cards and distribution. Remember, a hand containing 6 points
is a fair hand and a hand containing 9 points is a good hand. 8
points, therefore, would make a fairly good hand.

As South you hold:

(A)		(B)	
♠ A J x x x	(5)	♠ Q J x x x	(3)
♡ x x x		♡ x x x	
◇ Q x x	(2)	◇ K J x	(4)
♣ x x	(1)	♣ x x	(1)
	—		—
	8		8

The bidding has proceeded:

West	North	East	South
1 Club	Double	1 Heart	?

With either of these hands you should make a free bid of 1
Spade. You have 8 points—7 in high cards and 1 for distribution—so you have a hand which justifies a free bid at the level
of 1. If your free bid must be at a higher level you will require
slightly more strength.

As South you hold:

♠ A Q x x	(6)	
♡ x x	(1)	
◇ K x x x	(3)	
♣ x x x		
	—	
	10	

The bidding has proceeded:

West	North	East	South
1 Heart	Double	2 Hearts	?

Your hand has the value of 10 points, and you should make a
free bid of 2 Spades.

Raises by Doubler

The doubler should exercise caution in offering raises to a partner whom he has forced to bid.

As South you hold:

♠ A Q x x
♡ K Q x x
◇ x
♣ Q x x x

The bidding has proceeded:

East	South	West	North
1 Diamond	Double	Pass	1 Spade
Pass	?		

You should raise only to 2 Spades. Remember, partner may have no values.

The above hand was valued at 15 points when you doubled —13 in high cards and 2 for distribution. However, since partner has responded in a suit which you can well support, you may revalue your hand as dummy; the singleton, therefore, becomes worth 3 points in the dummy hand (whereas it would have been valued at only 2 points in the hand of the initial bidder).

The following is a reasonably accurate guide for a doubler who is contemplating a raise of his partner's forced take-out:

With 16 points he may go to the 2 level
With 19 points he may go to the 3 level
With 22 points he may go to the 4 level

Action by Opener's Partner Over a Double

Before proceeding any further into this subject let me caution you against a popular superstition to the effect that "a bid over a double shows weakness." It doesn't do so any more than it shows your political affiliation.

What you should do when partner's opening bid has been doubled depends on the type of hand you hold. Briefly, here is the practice:

With a good hand you redouble. This may be done even without support for partner's suit. What constitutes a good hand? One that is above average in high cards, or which, because of distribution, is worth more than one bid. Remember, so far as responder is concerned, the indifferent hands range from 6 to 10 points—when they are above that strength, responder has a good hand and must plan to bid more. He must, therefore, make a one round force. The redouble serves that purpose, and assures him another opportunity to bid. Unless the opposition is indiscreet enough to let the hand play at one redoubled, which should be a tasty enough morsel.

With a weak hand you *pass*, except that you are permitted to give partner a raise if adequate trump support is held, just to get into the other fellow's hair.

With hands of mediocre value (anything up to about 9 or 10 points), it is better strategy to bid early and avoid the rush.

Partner opens 1 Heart. Next hand doubles. You hold:

(1) ♠ A J x x   (2) ♠ x x
     ♡ x   ♡ J x x
     ◊ K J x x   ◊ A x x x x
     ♣ K J x x   ♣ K Q x

(3) ♠ x x   (4) ♠ x
     ♡ Q x x x   ♡ Q x x x x
     ◊ K x x x   ◊ K x x x x
     ♣ x x x   ♣ x x

          (5) ♠ A J x x x
               ♡ x x
               ◊ K x x
               ♣ x x x

(1) Redouble, though you have no support for partner's suit. Your hand is above average in high cards. In fact it has a value in high cards alone of 13 points.

(2) Redouble. In support of Hearts, this hand has a value of 11 points.

(3) Raise to 2 Hearts. This may be done on relatively weak holdings. This hand has a valuation of 7.

(4) Bid 3 Hearts—a barricade raise made in an attempt to embarrass the opposition. Such a bid usually shows about 8 to 10 points in support.

(5) Bid 1 Spade. This hand is not strong enough to redouble. It is worth only 9 points.

Conversely—as South you hold:

♠ A K 10 x
♡ x x x
◇ A K x
♣ x x x

The bidding has proceeded:

South	West	North	East
1 Spade	Double	3 Spades	Pass

What do you bid?
You should pass. Your hand has the value of 14 points. In order to produce game partner would have to contribute 12 points, which he has denied holding. If he had that many he would have redoubled. North is simply trying to make a pest of himself to the opponents and so far has succeeded.

IN BRIEF

A take-out double should be based on a hand of the same strength as an opening bid, that is, 13 points.

An immediate double of 1 No Trump should therefore be based on 16 points.

When partner responds in a suit for which you have good support, revalue your hand as dummy.

As responder to a take-out double: if you have 6 points you have a fair hand, 9 points a good hand, and 11 points a probable game.

As partner of the opening bidder, after a take-out double pass with a poor hand, redouble with a good hand, and bid immediately with a moderate hand.

CHAPTER XVII

PENALTY DOUBLES

THE POINT COUNT is not a complete guide for purposes of making penalty doubles in suit bids. But in making penalty doubles of No Trump contracts it may be applied with deadly accuracy.

In making these computations, when partner has opened with 1 of a suit, it is presumed that he has at least 13 points. By adding your values to those announced by partner, a rough estimate may be made of the comparative strength of the two teams.

Likewise at No Trump where your side outweighs the enemy by 4 or 5 points, you should be able to beat them at a 1 No Trump contract, since your side should win more tricks, e.g.,

Your partner opens 1 Spade. Right hand opponent overcalls with 1 No Trump. You hold:

♠ Q x x
♡ 10 x x x
◊ A J x
♣ K x x

Without even considering the promoted value of the Queen of Spades you have 10 points—13 + 10 = 23. You outweigh the enemy by at least 23 to 17 and a penalty double is in order.

It may be argued that a considerable portion of the opening bidder's 13 points may consist of distributional values—

that is, singletons and doubletons, which are not helpful in defense of No Trump contracts. The answer is that in such cases the opening bidder should realize that his hand is unsuitable defensively, and he should not stand for the double of a low contract, e.g.,

As South you hold:

♠ A Q x x x x x
♡ x x
◊ K J x
♣ x

The bidding has proceeded:

South	West	North	East
1 Spade	1 No Trump	Double	Pass
?			

You should rebid 2 Spades, since your hand is unsuitable defensively.

With a good five card suit you may double a 1 No Trump bid with a point less, e.g.,

Your partner opens 1 Spade. Right hand opponent overcalls with 1 No Trump. You hold:

♠ x x x
♡ x x
◊ x x x
♣ A K Q x x

You should double; $13 + 9 = 22$ (plus a five card suit). Opponents have at most 18.

A fairly accurate guide is this: When your partner opens the bidding and your right hand opponent overcalls with that suit which it was your desire to bid, double for keeps. The technique is to count the number of tricks you expect partner to produce. (Experience has shown that the normal opening bid of 1 in a suit will produce about three tricks in the defensive play.) Then on the fingers of your left hand count the number you expect to contribute, add them together, and "let her go."

As South you hold:

♠ x x
♡ A x x x
♢ K J 9 x
♣ x x x

The bidding has proceeded:

North	East	South
1 Spade	2 Diamonds	?

Double. You may expect to win three tricks in Diamonds and one in Hearts. The opener may be relied upon to develop three tricks. This comes to seven. A two trick penalty is anticipated. You must not fall into the error of calling 2 No Trump, with a hand that contains only 8 points in high cards.

QUIZZES

(Answers on pages 134 to 150)

QUIZ NO. 1

As dealer you hold the following hands. What is your opening bid?

(1) ♠ Q 10 7 4 3
    ♡ 2
    ◇ A K J 9 2
    ♣ K 8

(2) ♠ K Q J
    ♡ 9 8 7 6
    ◇ K J 5
    ♣ Q J 10

(3) ♠ Q 10 8 7
    ♡ K 10 7 5
    ◇ Q 3
    ♣ A Q 4

(4) ♠ 4 3 2
    ♡ A K
    ◇ A Q J 10
    ♣ K 5 4 3

(5) ♠ 7
    ♡ K J 10 7
    ◇ A Q 9 8 3
    ♣ A J 3

(6) ♠ 7 4 2
    ♡ 6 5
    ◇ A J 9 7 3
    ♣ A Q 5

(7) ♠ A K J 9 6
    ♡ A Q J
    ◇ A 7
    ♣ K J 10

(8) ♠ A 7 3
    ♡ A 9 5
    ◇ A Q 10 9 5
    ♣ A 8

(9) ♠ A K Q 6
    ♡ 8 3
    ◇ Q 10 7 5
    ♣ K 7 4

(10) ♠ A 6
    ♡ 10 7 6 5 3
    ◇ 7 2
    ♣ A K J 4

(11) ♠ A K Q 10 9 4 3
♥ K 7
♦ 4 3 2
♣ 6

(16) ♠ A
♥ Q 9 8 6
♦ Q 10 7 3
♣ A J 10 9

(12) ♠ A 10 6 4
♥ A K 10 3 2
♦ 7
♣ Q 4 3

(17) ♠ 7 6
♥ K Q J 10 3
♦ A K Q J 2
♣ A

(13) ♠ A Q 10 4 3
♥ A Q 10 7 5 2
♦ 6
♣ 4

(18) ♠ K Q 8 7 3
♥ 3
♦ K J 9 7 6 5 4
♣ none

(14) ♠ A J 4 3 2
♥ 6
♦ A K Q
♣ A K 4 2

(19) ♠ A J 10 3
♥ A Q 10 5
♦ A K J 4
♣ 5

(15) ♠ K Q 10 6
♥ J 9 7 5
♦ A K Q 10
♣ 2

(20) ♠ K 3
♥ A 7
♦ A K 2
♣ A K Q J 7 5

QUIZ NO. 2

Partner opens with 1 No Trump. You hold the following hands. What is your response?

(1) ♠ A 6 4 2
♡ K 10 5 3
◊ A 9 8
♣ 4 3

(2) ♠ 7 5 3
♡ K J 4
◊ K 10 6 5 4 2
♣ 9

(3) ♠ A 10 9 4 2
♡ J 8 6
◊ K 9 5
♣ 10 3

(4) ♠ K Q 10 9 7
♡ A
◊ Q 10 9 8
♣ 5 4 2

(5) ♠ Q 7 5
♡ K Q J 9
◊ 4 3 2
♣ K 9 7

(6) ♠ K Q 10 9 7 3
♡ A 10
◊ K Q J 2
♣ 7

(7) ♠ Q 9 8 7
♡ K 9 5 4
◊ 2
♣ 10 9 6 3

(8) ♠ J 8 7 2
♡ A Q 10 8 6 2
◊ 7 5
♣ 10

You open with 1 No Trump. Partner responds 2 Clubs. What is your rebid on each of the following hands?

(9) ♠ K 10 3
♡ K 9 2
◊ K 8
♣ A K J 7 6

(10) ♠ J 9 7 3
♡ A Q 8 5
◊ K Q 10
♣ A 10

(11) ♠ A J 9
♡ A 9 6 5
◊ K Q 7
♣ K 10 2

(12) ♠ K Q 10
♡ A Q
◊ K J 10 3
♣ Q 10 9 6

In the following hands, you are South and the bidding is as indicated. What is your bid?

(13) ♠ K 8 7
    ♡ A Q 10 6
    ♢ A 10 4
    ♣ K 9 8

S.	W.	N.	E.
1 NT	P.	2 H.	P.
?			

(17) ♠ Q 9 3
    ♡ A 10 7 6 5
    ♢ Q 8 4
    ♣ 3 2

N.	E.	S.	W.
1 NT	P.	2 C.	P.
2 S.	P.	?	

(14) ♠ A 10 5
    ♡ K Q 8 3
    ♢ A J 3
    ♣ Q 9 8

S.	W.	N.	E.
1 NT	P.	2 C.	P.
2 H.	P.	3 H.	P.
?			

(18) ♠ A Q 9 8
    ♡ K Q J 5
    ♢ A K Q
    ♣ A J

S.	W.	N.	E.
3 NT	P.	4 C.	P.
?			

(15) ♠ Q 6 4
    ♡ A J 10
    ♢ K Q 9 8
    ♣ A J 3

S.	W.	N.	E.
1 NT	P.	2 C.	P.
2 D.	P.	2 S.	P.
?			

(19) ♠ Q J 3 2
    ♡ 7
    ♢ 9 8 6 5
    ♣ A K 4 2

N.	E.	S.
1 NT	2 H.	?

(16) ♠ K J 10 3
    ♡ K J 7 4
    ♢ J 7 4 3
    ♣ Q

N.	E.	S.	W.
1 NT	P.	2 C.	P.
2 D.	P.	?	

(20) ♠ A J
    ♡ K J 9 6
    ♢ K Q J
    ♣ K 8 7 3

S.	W.	N.	E.
1 NT	2 S.	2 NT	P.
?			

QUIZ NO. 3

Partner opens with 1 Diamond. You hold the following hands. What is your response?

(1) ♠ 8 7
    ♡ Q 10 6 4
    ◊ A J 10 3 2
    ♣ 9 5

(4) ♠ K Q J 2
    ♡ 7 5
    ◊ Q 3
    ♣ A 10 4 3 2

(2) ♠ Q 5 2
    ♡ J 10 6
    ◊ 3
    ♣ A J 8 5 4 2

(5) ♠ K 6
    ♡ A 10 9
    ◊ Q J 10 3
    ♣ K J 10 6

(3) ♠ Q J 9 2
    ♡ K 7 4 3
    ◊ 10 7 3
    ♣ 8 6

(6) ♠ J 4 2
    ♡ A Q 9
    ◊ K 7 6 5 3
    ♣ 7 6

Partner opens with 1 Heart. You hold the following hands. What is your response?

(7) ♠ K 10 4 3 2
    ♡ A J 2
    ◊ 10 9 5
    ♣ 6 3

(10) ♠ Q 8 3
     ♡ A 7 5
     ◊ 4 2
     ♣ 10 8 7 4 3

(8) ♠ K 10 9 6
    ♡ Q J 9 3
    ◊ A K 4 2
    ♣ 7

(11) ♠ A K Q 10
     ♡ J 10 7 3
     ◊ 9 8 7 6
     ♣ 2

(9) ♠ 3
    ♡ 10 2
    ◊ K 10 9 6 4
    ♣ A 10 9 5 3

(12) ♠ A Q 8 7 2
     ♡ none
     ◊ A K J 2
     ♣ K J 9 6

In the following examples you are South and the bidding is as indicated. What is your bid?

(13) ♠ K Q 3
♡ 4 2
◇ A J 9 6 2
♣ 10 7 3

S.	N.
P.	1 S.
?	

(14) ♠ 7
♡ A 9 8 3 2
◇ K Q J 9 2
♣ 10 6

S.	N.
P.	1 H.
?	

(15) ♠ Q 3
♡ 10 7
◇ 10 8 6 5 4
♣ A J 4 3

N.	S.
2 S.	?

(16) ♠ 6
♡ K 10 8 7 2
◇ 7
♣ Q 10 6 5 4 2

N.	E.	S.
1 S.	2 H.	?

(17) ♠ K J 3
♡ A Q 8 7 6
◇ 10 5
♣ 9 6 3

N.	E.	S.
1 D.	1 S.	?

(18) ♠ A
♡ 6 2
◇ K 8 7 6 5 3
♣ K Q 10 2

N.	E.	S.
1 D.	1 S.	?

(19) ♠ Q 10 2
♡ 7 6 3
◇ K 9 5
♣ Q 7 6 3

N.	S.
1 C.	?

(20) ♠ 7
♡ K Q 8 3
◇ K Q 10 6
♣ K J 3 2

N.	S.
3 S.	?

QUIZ NO. 4

Holding the following hands, you open the bidding with 1 Club. Partner responds 1 Heart. What is your rebid?

(1) ♠ A Q 4 3
♡ K J 5
◇ 7 3
♣ A Q 10 3

(3) ♠ J 10 5
♡ 10 4 2
◇ A Q
♣ A Q J 9 8

(2) ♠ K J 8 5
♡ 7
◇ K 2
♣ A K 10 4 3 2

(4) ♠ 3
♡ K 7 2
◇ A Q 9 5
♣ A K 10 9 6

Holding the following hands, you open the bidding with 1 Heart. Partner responds 1 No Trump. What is your rebid?

(5) ♠ 7
♡ A K 10 9 2
◇ 7 5 2
♣ K Q 8 7

(6) ♠ A Q 10
♡ A K J 10 3
◇ 2
♣ K Q 10 5

Holding the following hands, you open the bidding with 1 Spade. Partner raises to 2 Spades. What is your rebid?

(7) ♠ A 10 8 7 3
♡ K Q 9 5
◇ A Q
♣ 3 2

(8) ♠ K Q 9 6 2
♡ 7
◇ A K
♣ A K 5 4 3

In the following examples you are South and the bidding is as indicated. What is your bid?

(9) ♠ A J 10 4 3
    ♡ 8 6
    ◇ A K J 10
    ♣ 5 2

S.	N.
1 S.	2 H.
?	

(12) ♠ 10 8 6 4
     ♡ A K 4 2
     ◇ A 7
     ♣ A 8 3

S.	W.	N.	E.
1 C.	P.	2 C.	P.
?			

(10) ♠ Q 4 3
     ♡ 7
     ◇ A Q J 9 3
     ♣ A Q J 2

S.	N.
1 D.	1 S.
?	

(13) ♠ A 7 5 4
     ♡ K 9 3 2
     ◇ A K Q 4
     ♣ A

S.	W.	N.	E.
1 D.	P.	1 NT	P.
?			

(11) ♠ A K Q 9 8
     ♡ K 10 6
     ◇ J 4 2
     ♣ 7 2

S.	W.	N.	E.
1 S.	P.	2 C.	2 D.
?			

(14) ♠ K J 3
     ♡ K J 8 3
     ◇ A 10 5 2
     ♣ K 5

S.	W.	N.	E.
1 H.	1 S.	2 D.	P.
?			

QUIZ NO. 5

You are South in each of the following problems and the bidding is as indicated. What is your rebid?

(1) ♠ 4 3 2
   ♡ K 10 7 6 3
   ♢ A J 10
   ♣ 6 5

N.	S.
1 D.	1 H.
2 H.	?

(2) ♠ Q 9 3
   ♡ K J 6 3
   ♢ Q 10 8 7 3
   ♣ 2

N.	S.
1 D.	1 H.
1 S.	?

(3) ♠ 6 3 2
   ♡ K J 10 6 4 3
   ♢ 7 4
   ♣ A K

N.	S.
1 D.	1 H.
1 NT	?

(4) ♠ A 6 3
   ♡ J 10 4 3 2
   ♢ 9
   ♣ Q 10 9 5

N.	S.
1 D.	1 H.
2 NT	?

(5) ♠ 8 6 5
   ♡ A Q J 3
   ♢ 7 5
   ♣ K Q 9 5

N.	S.
1 D.	1 H.
2 C.	?

(6) ♠ K 5 2
   ♡ Q J 9 6 2
   ♢ none
   ♣ 9 8 7 4 3

N.	S.
1 D.	1 H.
2 D.	?

(7) ♠ Q 8 6
   ♡ 4 2
   ♢ K 4 3
   ♣ A Q 9 5 2

N.	S.
1 S.	2 C.
2 NT	?

(8) ♠ J 8 7 3
   ♡ J 2
   ♢ A 9 8 6
   ♣ K 5 2

N.	S.
1 D.	2 D.
3 D.	?

(9) ♠ 7
♥ K 8 6 4
♦ A J 10 5 4
♣ 6 3 2

N.	S.
1 S.	1 NT
2 H.	?

(12) ♠ K 10 6 4 3
♥ 4
♦ J 8
♣ K 9 8 7 5

N.	S.
1 H.	1 S.
1 NT	?

(10) ♠ K 7 5
♥ K 8 7 6
♦ Q 10 3
♣ 4 3 2

N.	S.
1 C.	1 H.
1 S.	?

(13) ♠ K 10 7 3
♥ K 8 2
♦ K 9 4
♣ 7 3 2

N.	E.	S.	W.
1 S.	2 C.	2 S.	P.
3 S.	P.	?	

(11) ♠ Q 10 6 3
♥ Q 4 2
♦ K 9 7
♣ 5 4 2

N.	S.
1 D.	1 S.
2 H.	?

(14) ♠ Q 10 9 6
♥ A K 8 2
♦ 7 5
♣ 9 7 3

N.	E.	S.
1 D.	2 C.	?

QUIZ NO. 6

Your right hand opponent has opened with 1 Heart. What do you bid on the following hands?

(1) ♠ A Q 8 3
♡ 7 4 2
◊ A K J 9 2
♣ 7

(5) ♠ A K Q 7 4 3 2
♡ 6 5
◊ 2
♣ A J 10

(2) ♠ A
♡ A K J 9
◊ Q 5 4
♣ K 10 9 6 2

(6) ♠ A J 10 9 7 3 2
♡ 8 6
◊ 7 5
♣ 9 4

(3) ♠ K Q 8 7 5 2
♡ J
◊ none
♣ A Q J 9 7 3

(7) ♠ K Q 10 6 3
♡ J 7 6 4 3
◊ A
♣ 9 6

(4) ♠ K 7
♡ A Q 10
◊ A K J 4 2
♣ K J 3

(8) ♠ K Q 4 3
♡ 7
◊ Q J 10 9 8 6 2
♣ 5

In the following problems, you are South and the bidding is as indicated. What is your bid?

West	North	East	South
1 Diamond	Double	Pass	?

(9) ♠ 4 3 2
♡ J 10 6
◊ A J 9 7
♣ 5 3 2

(10) ♠ Q 4 3 2
♡ J 6
◊ 7 5
♣ K 10 9 8 6

(11) ♠ K 10 5 4
      ♡ 7 4 3
      ◇ K Q 7 3
      ♣ K 2

(12) ♠ 2
      ♡ Q J 9 8 6 5
      ◇ 4 3
      ♣ A 10 7 6

In the following problems you are South and the bidding is as indicated. What is your bid?

(13) ♠ A Q 5 2
      ♡ K J 4 2
      ◇ 6 3
      ♣ A J 5

E.	S.	W.	N.
1 D.	Do.	P.	1 S.
3 D.	?		

(14) ♠ K J 8 3 2
      ♡ 6 4 3
      ◇ Q 10 4
      ♣ 6 2

W.	N.	E.	S.
1 H.	Do.	3 H.	?

(15) ♠ none
      ♡ K J 10 7
      ◇ 8 4 3
      ♣ A 10 9 8 6 5

N.	E.	S.
1 H.	Do.	?

(16) ♠ 2
      ♡ 7 6 5 4 2
      ◇ A 10 6 3
      ♣ K 9 5

N.	E.	S.
1 S.	Do.	?

(17) ♠ 6
      ♡ 5
      ◇ K Q 10 9 2
      ♣ A J 9 8 3 2

W.	N.	E.	S.
1 S.	P.	3 S.	?

(18) ♠ 7 4 3
      ♡ K Q 6 2
      ◇ K J 9 5
      ♣ K 4

W.	N.	E.	S.
1 H.	2 S.	3 H.	?

(19) ♠ J 10 5
      ♡ A 10 7 6 2
      ◇ K J 5 2
      ♣ 7

East	South	West	North
1 H.	P.	1 NT	2 NT
P.	?		

(20) ♠ 7 4 3
      ♡ A J
      ◇ K 10 6 5 4
      ♣ K J 7

North	East	South
1 D.	3 C.	?

(21) ♠ K 8
      ♡ A 9 5
      ◇ Q 7 3
      ♣ 7 6 5 4 2

N.	E.	S.
1 NT	3 S.	?

QUIZ NO. 7

You are South in each of the following problems and the bidding is as indicated. What action do you take?

(1) ♠ A 7 3
♥ A K J 10 3
♦ 4 2
♣ A 10 5

S.	W.	N.	E.
1 H.	P.	3 H.	P.
?			

(2) ♠ 5
♥ A 10 6 2
♦ K Q 7 3
♣ A K 9 2

N.	E.	S.
3 D.	P.	?

(3) ♠ 2
♥ A K Q 10 9 8
♦ A K 2
♣ A 8 4

S.	W.	N.	E.
2 H.	P.	3 H.	P.
?			

(4) ♠ A Q J 3 2
♥ A K 10 9 6 4
♦ 8 5
♣ none

S.	W.	N.	E.
1 H.	P.	1 S.	P.
?			

(5) ♠ K 6 2
♥ A 7 5
♦ A K 8 3 2
♣ 4 3

N.	E.	S.	W.
P.	P.	1 D.	P.
3 C.	P.	3 D.	P.
5 D.	P.	?	

(6) ♠ K 5
♥ none
♦ A Q 10 5 4
♣ Q 9 8 7 4 3

N.	E.	S.	W.
1 D.	P.	3 D.	P.
4 NT	P.	?	

(7) ♠ none
♥ K Q J 4 3 2
♦ K J 5 3 2
♣ A 10

N.	E.	S.
1 C.	1 S.	?

(8) ♠ A Q J 8 7
♥ 3 2
♦ 7
♣ A Q 9 8 7

S.	W.	N.	E.
1 S.	P.	3 S.	P.
4 C.	P.	4 H.	P.
4 S.	P.	5 D.	Do.
?			

(9) ♠ A 7 4 2
  ♡ Q 6
  ◇ 7 5
  ♣ K Q 8 4 3

N.	E.	S.	W.
1 D.	P.	2 C.	P.
2 D.	2 H.	?	

(12) ♠ A
  ♡ J 4 3
  ◇ A 10 8 5 2
  ♣ Q 7 4 3

N.	E.	S.	W.
1 S.	2 D.	Do.	P.
3 S.	P.	3 NT	P.
4 H.	P.	?	

(10) ♠ K 8 4 3
  ♡ 6 2
  ◇ A 10 6 2
  ♣ 7 5 3

N.	E.	S.	W.
1 S.	2 H.	2 S.	3 H.
4 S.	5 H.	?	

(13) ♠ K 8 7 6 3
  ♡ A J 9 4 3
  ◇ 6
  ♣ A 7

W.	N.	E.	S.
1 D.	2 C.	P.	?

(11) ♠ K 8 6 4
  ♡ Q 10 8 3
  ◇ 7
  ♣ K 7 5 2

W.	N.	E.	S.
1 D.	2 D.	4 D.	?

(14) ♠ Q 8 4 3
  ♡ 10 5
  ◇ J 3
  ♣ Q J 8 7 2

W.	N.	E.	S.
1 H.	P.	1 S.	P.
2 H.	Do.	P.	?

ANSWERS To QUIZ No. 1

1. 1 Spade. This hand is worth 16 points, 13 in high cards and 3 for distribution. With two five card suits, the higher ranking is chosen to start the bidding despite the fact that the lower ranking contains the greater strength.

2. Pass. This hand contains only 12 points since 1 point must be subtracted for the lack of Aces when one is considering an opening bid. 13 points is the minimum requirement for an opening bid.

3. 1 Club. This hand, containing 14 points, is a mandatory opening. The Club bid is chosen for convenience since neither major suit is biddable according to current standards which require 4 points in high cards for an opening call in a major. After the 1 Club opening you have a convenient 1 Heart rebid if partner responds 1 Diamond, or you can offer him a raise if he names a major himself.

4. 1 No Trump is the most descriptive call on this balanced holding of 17 high card points. The three small Spades should not be a deterrent since it is permissible to have one suit completely unstopped provided it has at least three card length.

5. 1 Heart. This hand has a value of 17 points and, although it is well above a minimum, it is best to plan on showing both suits at a reasonable level. This may be done only by pretending that the Hearts and Diamonds are of the same length.

6. Pass. This hand is worth only 12 points which leaves it 1 point short of the minimum requirement for an opening bid in the first or second position. In third seat, a bid of 1 Diamond would be in order.

7. 2 No Trump. This hand falls a shade short of the requirements for a demand bid. However, it does contain 23 high card points with all suits stopped and, as such, comes within the range of a 2 No Trump opening.

8. 1 Diamond. Possession of all four Aces brings this hand up to 19 points, too much for 1 No Trump. 19 or 20-point hands are usually best handled by an opening bid in a suit, with a jump in No Trump reserved for the rebid.

9. 1 Diamond. With two or more four card suits, the opening bidder should select the first biddable suit below the doubleton—or singleton. Since the 4 high card point requirement applies only to the major, the Diamond suit may be regarded as biddable.

134

10. 1 Club. For reasons of convenience, it is advisable to treat the Hearts and Clubs as if they were the same length. If you open with 1 Heart and partner's response is 2 Diamonds, you will find yourself in a very uncomfortable position.

11. The proper opening is 1 Spade. This hand is too strong for preemptive bid, even at the game level.

12. 1 Heart. It would be improper to open this hand with 1 Spade. The only time two adjacent suits can be treated as being of the same length is when the four card suit has texture equal to the five card suit. Your Hearts are much better than the Spades. You should therefore open with 1 Heart, and over 2 Diamonds, rebid 2 Hearts.

13. 1 Spade. This hand is a minimum in high card strength and the suits are of similar texture. They should accordingly be treated as equals to conserve bidding strength. You plan subsequently to bid and rebid the Hearts.

14. 1 Spade. This hand is worth 23 points and is a little short of the requirements for a demand bid—25 points with a five card suit.

15. 1 Spade, the first biddable suit below the singleton.

16. 1 Diamond. Although Hearts is the first suit below the singleton, your Heart holding is not regarded as biddable. A four card major suit must contain at least 4 high card points in order to be biddable.

17. 2 Hearts. This hand falls microscopically short of the technical requirements for a demand bid, but the requirements may be shaded a trifle when your suits have such excellent texture. This holding will probably produce a game, facing a complete Yarborough.

18. Pass. Although this hand counts up to 13 points, it does not constitute an acceptable opening bid because of the lack of sufficient defensive values. Remember, these hands must have 2 quick tricks in order to qualify.

19. 1 Diamond. An exception to the general rule for handling four card suits is to be noted when you have 20 points or more. In such instances, the cheapest opening bid should be selected to facilitate a response from partner. If he should have some very weak hand containing a Heart suit, he might be willing to show it in response to an opening Diamond bid, whereas an opening in Spades might elicit a pass.

20. 3 No Trump. While this hand contains 1 point less than the standard requirement for this call, the deficiency is atoned for by possession of a solid six card suit. The objection to a demand bid in Clubs is that partner's expected 2 No Trump response may subject your Spade suit to an opening assault with possibly disastrous results.

ANSWERS To QUIZ No. 2

1. 2 Clubs. This hand may play better in a suit contract should partner have one of the majors. If his rebid is either 2 Spades or 2 Hearts you will raise to 4. If he denies a major, you will jump to 3 No Trump.

2. 2 No Trump. You have 7 points, a good six card suit and no special interest in the majors. Do not bid 2 Diamonds, a bid which partner will almost surely pass.

3. 2 Clubs. An alternate call would be a raise to 2 No Trump. But in view of the fact that the hand might conceivably play better at Spades, the 2 Club response gives you two chances. If partner's rebid is 2 Diamonds or 2 Hearts you will show the Spades. Your 2 Spade bid in this sequence will not be forcing. Partner has the option to pass or go on in either Spades or No Trump.

4. 3 Spades. We do not recommend the use of the 2 Club bid in this case. Obviously it is your intention to reach game. The 3 Spade response is forcing. If partner raises that suit you will be happy with the contract. If partner rebids 3 No Trump that should be the best spot.

5. 3 No Trump. The 2 Club Convention ought not to be used on an evenly distributed holding. This hand will probably produce the same number of tricks in No Trump as it would in Hearts even if your partner has four.

6. 4 Clubs, the ideal holding on which to use the Gerber Convention. Your sole interest is in how many controls partner has. If his No Trump bid includes just one Ace, you will stay out of a slam; if he has two Aces, you will bid 6 Spades; and if he has three, you may explore the possibility of a grand slam by asking for Kings.

7. Pass. It is not safe to employ the 2-Club Convention even though the hand might play better in a suit. Should partner's rebid be 2 Diamonds, you might find subsequent action very hazardous.

8. 4 Hearts, showing a good six card suit with less than 10 points in high cards. Your Hearts are self-sustaining facing an opening 1 No Trump bid, so there is no need to find out if partner has Spades.

9. 2 Diamonds. This response is automatic when you have no biddable major. If partner now names a major suit himself you can raise him.

10. 2 Hearts. With a holding in both majors the correct procedure is to bid Spades first. However, since the Spade suit in the present holding is not a biddable one, you have little choice but to show the Hearts instead.

11. 2 Hearts. The response to 2 Clubs is automatic. There is no such thing as an initial rebid of 2 No Trump by opener when his partner is using the convention.

12. 2 Diamonds. The same comment applies here as in problem #11. Your partner is in charge and at this point all he wants you to tell him is whether or not you have a biddable major.

13. Pass. Any response of 2 in a suit other than 2 Clubs is a weakness bid and requests the opener to pass. You have a minimum No Trump with even distribution. Therefore, you have no basis for further action despite the fit.

14. Pass. You have a minimum No Trump and partner's raise is not forcing. Had he wished to play a game opposite 16 points, he would have proceeded to 4 himself.

15. 2 No Trump. Partner's bid is not forcing. However, you have better than a minimum with a fitting card in his suit. The No Trump rebid is preferred to a Spade raise, though partner is marked with a five card suit, because of your evenly balanced distribution and secure stoppers in the other suits.

16. 3 No Trump. Partner has denied a biddable major and any suit bid by you at this point would show at least five card length. Don't bid 2 No Trump as this call could be passed.

17. 2 No Trump. Do not bid 3 Hearts which would be forcing to game. When the 2 Club bidder shows his suit at the level of 3 the bid is absolutely forcing. This hand contains the elements of a raise to 2 No Trump, and since partner's rebid has deprived you of the opportunity to explore for a Heart fit at a convenient level, you must return to No Trump.

18. 4 No Trump, showing three Aces. An immediate response of 4 Clubs over an opening bid of 1, 2 or 3 No Trump is Gerber and asks for Aces.

19. East has deprived you of the opportunity to use the 2-Club Convention. However, it is still possible to explore for a possible Spade fit via a false cue bid in the opponent's suit—3 Hearts. While this call normally announces first round control, we have found it expedient to adopt a more flexible attitude and use the bid as a game forcing device, despite the absence of first round control. In the present instance, if partner has a Spade suit, he will show it; if not, he will return to 3 No Trump.

20. 3 Hearts. You have the values to proceed to game. However, you should stop off first to check on the possibilities of a Heart fit. Partner could easily have a four card suit that he was unable to show over the adverse overcall. Note, too, that partner was deprived of the opportunity to employ the 2-Club Convention.

ANSWERS To QUIZ No. 3

1. 1 Heart. Despite your excellent Diamond fit, the opportunity to show a major suit at the level of 1 should not be by-passed. The Diamond support may be shown later, if it proves expedient to do so.

2. 1 No Trump. Though this hand contains 10 points counting high cards and distribution, it is not wise to carry the bidding into the 2 level. If partner is unable to carry on over 1 No Trump, little will be lost.

3. 1 Heart. If this hand possessed greater high card strength, we would recommend bidding your suits in normal order, but since you plan on making only one constructive bid, it is best to show the Hearts. Your partner will then be in position conveniently to raise you or show a Spade suit himself, should he fit one of the majors.

4. 2 Clubs. This holding is strong enough to be bid naturally. Cheapness is never recommended for its own sake. In fact, an initial response of 1 Spade is liable to wind up being more expensive, for if partner rebids 2 Diamonds, it would become necessary to enter the 3 level to show your second suit.

5. 2 No Trump. This response has the advantage of describing your holding in one bid (13-15 points in high cards and all unbid suits stopped). There is nothing to be gained, therefore, by a temporizing call of 2 Clubs. The 2 No Trump bid is preferable to a jump in Diamonds.

6. Although 1 No Trump is technically correct, we recommend the somewhat unorthodox call of 1 Heart, as though one of the small Diamonds were a heart. This bid will permit more convenient exploration for a possible game contract. Partner might pass 1 No Trump on some hand that could produce 9 tricks. If, over 1 Heart, he rebids 1 No Trump, you will be in position to raise to 2.

7. 2 Hearts. This is a mediocre hand worth only one constructive bid. Accordingly, a raise of partner's major is preferred to bidding your own suit.

8. 1 Spade. This hand is worth 17 points in support of Hearts and slightly exceeds the bounds of a jump raise. You must, therefore, make a temporizing bid initially with the expectation of making another constructive bid before supporting Hearts.

9. 1 No Trump. With 7 points in high cards, you should keep the bidding open. Since this holding is not strong enough to project the bidding into the 2 level, 1 No Trump is the only available response.

10. 1 No Trump. Since this hand is worth only 6 points in support of Hearts, it is not quite good enough to offer an immediate raise. 1 No Trump is the indicated bid.

11. 3 Hearts describes your hand in one bid, (14 points in support of Hearts including high cards and distribution).

12. 1 Spade. Although this hand is valued at 21 points, a jump shift is not recommended. On holdings where no fit is apparent, it is best to leave plenty of room open for exploration purposes. You are in position to show all three of your suits conveniently, if you don't crowd the bidding initially.

13. 2 Spades. Don't bid 2 Diamonds. Since you have passed originally, a bid in a new suit is no longer forcing, and partner is more apt to be encouraged by a raise in his suit.

14. Although 4 Hearts is acceptable, the recommended bid is 3 Diamonds. The jump in a new suit by a passed hand is forcing for one round and represents the most convenient method of probing for a possible slam. This holding is worth 14 points in support of Hearts, so a raise to 3, which is not forcing, would be considered totally inadequate.

15. 3 Spades. An opening demand bid is based on at least a good five card suit, so that the Queen, small, constitutes acceptable support. Furthermore, there is no convenient alternative, since the Diamond suit is too shabby to show. A bid in that denomination could only be misleading.

16. Pass. While it is tempting to double, such action is not recommended. It is almost a certainty that the bid will be rescued, and if partner doubles subsequently, depending on you to take defensive tricks, your proper course of action will not be at all clear.

17. 1 No Trump. This hand is not strong enough to show the Hearts, as such action may catapult the bidding into the 3 level. However, some offensive action is indicated, and a free bid of 1 No Trump will fill the bill. Partner will know you have a hand of at least average strength with Spade protection.

18. 2 Spades. On strong hands it is usually best to make a display of strength below the game level. The cue bid of the opponent's suit is unconditionally forcing to game, and after you show the Diamond support on the next round, you will be in position to relax and leave any subsequent forward moves to partner.

19. 2 Clubs. Despite the balanced nature of this holding, a 1 No Trump bid is not available, since that response to a 1 Club opening is reserved for hands of greater strength (9-11 high card points). 1 Diamond is an acceptable alternative, but the immediate raise is less apt to complicate matters later.

20. Pass. While you have a sound opening bid, your values do not include the right material to produce a game opposite a pre-emptive opening in Spades. A great big demerit for a response of 3 No Trump.

ANSWERS To QUIZ No. 4

1. 1 Spade. When we have opened the bidding we prefer, wherever possible, to avoid making an immediate raise of partner's suit with only three trumps. This hand presents a convenient rebid of 1 Spade which will offer partner an opportunity to clarify his holding.

2. 1 Spade. Possession of a six card minor suit does not constitute sufficient reason for by-passing the chance to show a major at the level of 1.

3. 1 No Trump. This is a balanced holding of minimum proportions. Do not rebid 2 Clubs merely to show a five card suit. 1 No Trump is much more descriptive of your holding.

4. 2 Diamonds. This is an indirect way of describing the strength of your hand. You have the values for a jump raise in Hearts but lack the fourth Heart which is a prerequisite for such action. The 2 Diamond bid, a technical reverse, will announce a holding of 18 or 19 points. On the next round you will support Hearts.

5. Your hand is unbalanced and an effort should be made to play in a suit contract. This effort should take the form of a 2 Club rebid. Your partner will be offered a choice of contracts and he may easily have a distinct preference for Clubs.

6. 3 Clubs. You have 21 points and should insist on a game contract once partner is able to keep the bidding open.

7. Your hand revalues to 18 points when partner raises Spades which means that a game should be available if he has a fair holding. A bid of either 3 Spades or 3 Hearts would be considered acceptable. However, our preference runs toward the latter choice, since partner might have a hand containing four Hearts in which case the Spades could be used for discards from the dummy.

8. Nothing less than a jump to 4 Clubs would be adequate. Slam prospects would be very bright if partner has four trumps, an Ace and either short Clubs or the Queen.

9. 2 Spades. This is a minimum opening bid and you must do nothing to give partner any contrary impression. A bid of 3 Diamonds at this stage would show a much better hand.

10. 2 Clubs. This hand would qualify as a jump raise if you had one more Spade. Lacking that card, you have no choice but to make a temporizing rebid hoping to coax another call from partner. You will then be in position to give a delayed raise.

11. Pass. A 2 Spade bid at this point would be the act of a road hog. Partner promised a fair hand when he took the bidding into the 2 level, and you should defer the proceedings to him. His action will serve to clarify the situation considerably. If he is able to double the opposition, they may live to regret their indiscretion.

12. Pass. There is no future in this hand. A game can no longer be in contemplation after partner's raise, nor is there likely to be a better contract, since he was unable to show any suit at the level of 1.

13. 3 No Trump. You have the values (20 high card points) to insist upon a game contract, and since partner by-passed both majors to respond in No Trump, the chances are good that he has some acceptable Club holding.

14. 2 No Trump. You have adequate trump support with which to raise partner. However, in view of your holdings in the other suits, the No Trump rebid appears to be the wiser choice. A 9 trick contract will most likely be much easier to make.

ANSWERS To QUIZ No. 5

1. 3 Hearts. This hand had an original valuation of 9 points, but now that Hearts have been supported, it is worth 10 when a point is added for the fifth Heart. It is true that partner would need a maximum raise to bring your total to 26, but in view of the Diamond fit, your points are of such good quality that you should be willing to reach for game with only 25 points.

2. 2 Diamonds. This is admittedly an underbid, but no convenient call is available. A game forcing jump to 3 Diamonds would not be temperate with only 8 high card points. A possible alternate call is 2 Spades which has the attraction of sounding more encouraging, although we hesitate recommending a raise of partner's secondary suit with only three trumps.

3. 3 Hearts. This hand is somewhat unbalanced and may play better at Hearts. At any rate you should throw your weight in that direction.

4. 3 No Trump. Despite the singleton Diamond, No Trump appears to be the most convenient game available. If another try for a suit contract is to be made, a 3 Club call is definitely preferred to rebidding the shabby Heart suit.

5. 3 Clubs. You have the values required to offer a jump raise, but a slight underbid is recommended to prevent the bidding from going past the 3 No Trump level. That contract could easily prove to be the only game available and partner should be offered the choice.

6. Pass. You kept the bidding open once with 6 points and partner's rebid has done nothing to promote your holding. Any further action is attended with great danger.

7. 3 Spades. There is no doubt that you are going to play this hand in game, but the Spade support should be shown at this point to offer partner a choice of contracts. The 3 Spade bid should not be interpreted as a sign-off since you made a constructive response initially.

8. 3 No Trump. Partner has shown an interest in game in the face of your weak response. 3 No Trump is probably your best chance even though it involves a slight gamble as regards the Heart suit.

9. 4 Hearts. In support of Hearts, this hand revalues to 12 points, enough to insist upon a game contract once the fit is established.

10. 1 No Trump. When used as a rebid by the responder, this call does not promise any extra values, and may be done with 8 or 9 points to give partner an opportunity to clarify the nature of his opening bid.

11. 3 Diamonds, a normal preference for partner's first suit. Have no fears about carrying the bidding into the 3 level, since partner guarantees a fine hand when he bids his suits in reverse order.

12. 2 Clubs. A bid of a new suit after partner has limited his opening with a 1 No Trump rebid is no longer forcing. It is, therefore, completely safe to probe further with an unbalanced holding of mediocre strength.

13. Pass. You told your story with the initial free raise. If there were a game available on this hand, partner would have to be able to bid it himself.

14. Pass. A free bid in a higher ranking suit at the 2 level should be based on a hand of about opening bid strength. This holding does not come close.

ANSWERS To QUIZ No. 6

1. **Double.** This is superior to an overcall of 2 Diamonds because it offers the additional chance that the hand may be played in Spades if partner has some length in that suit. If he bids 2 Clubs, you have a convenient retreat to Diamonds.

2. **Pass.** Whenever you are top-heavy in the opponent's suit, it is advisable to pass for one round and await developments. Maybe the opponents will talk themselves into serious trouble. A 1 No Trump bid is not recommended with a singleton Spade, and not enough is to be gained by bidding 2 Clubs.

3. **2 Clubs.** This is a slightly unorthodox overcall, but one dictated by convenience. It may prove easier to show both suits by calling Clubs initially. The bidding is very likely to reach 4 Hearts by the time it gets back to you, and a bid of 4 Spades at that point will present partner with a choice of suits at the most economical level.

4. **2 No Trump.** This bid best serves to describe your holding. Although the hand counts to only 21 high card points, there is compensation in the form of a very good five card suit, plus three potential stoppers in the opponent's suit. Note that an overcall in No Trump immediately over the opening bid is a natural call and not a request for the minors.

5. **Double.** You have a hand that will produce a game if partner has a couple of fitting cards. A mere overcall would be inadequate and a jump bid would be pre-emptive. The double followed by a jump in Spades is the only way to reveal your true strength.

6. **2 Spades,** a pre-emptive call. This is an ideal holding for a jump overcall. You have deprived the opponents of one level of bidding space and at the same time described your hand to partner. Further action is strictly up to him.

7. **1 Spade.** You have length in the opener's suit, but your strength is concentrated elsewhere and immediate action is recommended while the level of the bidding is low.

8. **2 Diamonds.** Pre-emptive bids should be avoided on holdings containing a secondary suit. A jump to 3 Diamonds might serve to block your side out of a fit in Spades and a possible game. Over 2 Diamonds, partner will mention a reasonable Spade holding, which he is unlikely to do if you announce that your hand is strictly one suited.

9. 1 Heart, not 1 No Trump. The 1 No Trump response to a take-out double is treated as a forward-going bid and should never be employed as a form of rescue. This occasionally necessitates responses in a three card suit. It is usually preferable to make the cheapest possible response, to allow partner greater space for landing purposes.

10. 1 Spade. A four card major is generally preferred to a five card minor in responding to a take-out double, for the doubler is frequently more interested in the majors.

11. 2 Spades. It is more important to show a major suit holding than the Diamond stoppers. If partner raises to 3 Spades, you will be in position to try 3 No Trump on the next round.

12. 4 Hearts. This hand rates to be in game facing a take-out double and your suit requires only the barest of support. 2 Hearts is an alternate choice but has the disadvantage of permitting the opposition to probe conveniently for the Spade fit they are very likely to have.

13. Pass. To bid freely at this level, with a partner who may have a bust, might prove suicidal. Remember, you forced partner to make his initial call.

14. 3 Spades. While you are a shade shy of the values to make a free bid at this level, such action should nevertheless be taken, else partner may be forced to pass for fear that you have nothing.

15. We recommend a leap to 4 Hearts as the best tactics. The opposition may have a game available in the other major and you should try to crowd them out of the bidding. If West bids 4 Spades anyway, and your partner passes, you may choose to show the Clubs on the next round.

16. Pass. Any thought of rescuing partner would be based on nothing more than panic. West is not likely to pass the double, and if he does, your hand will produce a trick or two as dummy.

17. 3 No Trump. East-West are surely headed for at least a game contract, and you have available a relatively cheap method for suggesting a possible save in one of the minors via the Unusual No Trump Overcall. Note that your call is not a natural one as it comes after both opponents have bid.

18. Pass. Partner has made a pre-emptive bid and cannot be counted on for any high card strength. Your hand does not figure to prove of much assistance to him and your best chance for a profit is to stay out of the proceedings.

19. 4 Diamonds. Partner is obviously making an Unusual No Trump Overcall requesting a minor suit. You have a very fine hand for his purposes, and prospects for game are bright. You should, therefore, show your interest by bidding one more than is necessary.

20. 3 No Trump. East's pre-empt has produced a strapping effect, since a free bid of just 3 Diamonds would sound like a mere competitive effort. You have the Clubs well stopped and it is reasonable under the circumstances to assume that partner has some values in Spades. If he can't stand No Trump, you will be able to support Diamonds subsequently.

21. Double, for a sure profit. Game may or may not be available but rather than speculate on a doubtful 3 No Trump, a quick appraisal of the partnership assets will reveal that you can contribute at least two defensive tricks to the four partner has indicated by his No Trump opening. This adds up to a minimum of a two trick set and the profit could easily be greater.

ANSWERS To QUIZ No. 7

1. 3 Spades. Prospects for slam are good. Your hand becomes worth 18 points when Hearts have been supported and partner may have as many as 16. On relatively balanced holdings, however, it is better to show Aces individually. If you use Blackwood, partner's response will leave you no more certain as to what the exact limits of the hand are. A worthless doubleton is usually a deterrent to the use of Blackwood.

2. 6 Diamonds. In terms of tricks, your hand should produce enough for a slam, and unless your partner's values badly duplicate yours in the form of a singleton Spade and several small Hearts, six should be a laydown. This would be impossible to determine through scientific investigation in any event, so you might just as well up and bid 6.

3. 4 Hearts. You have already told your story when you opened with a demand bid. Partner heard the opening bid and the fact that you sign off at this point does not prevent him from proceeding further if he has appropriate values.

4. This is the type of holding that defies a scientific approach. Six or seven may be a laydown or you could be off two quick tricks. Our recommendation is to seize the initiative while it is available and bid 6 Spades. That will put the burden on the opponents to find the killing defense if there is one.

5. 6 Diamonds. Despite the fact that partner passed originally and that you have a more or less minimum opening, the hands obviously fit well enough to produce a slam. Partner has something like ♠ x ♡ x ◇ J x x x x ♣ A K J x x x for his bid and your values are clearly the right ones.

6. We recommend the rather unorthodox response of 6 Diamonds. If you show one Ace, partner may pass, fearing that no slam is available when you have but a single control. This is actually not the case, and we feel that as long as partner is able to leap into Blackwood after our jump raise, we wish to reach at least a small slam.

7. 2 Hearts. While you have the values to insist on game via an immediate cue bid, such action is not recommended where you have a great deal to tell partner and no sure fit has as yet been discovered. The best procedure is to plan on showing both suits first and reserve the cue in Spades for such time as partner supports Diamonds or Hearts or shows a good rebiddable suit of his own.

8. The conventional procedure is to redouble. This announces a second round control of Diamonds (since Spades are obviously the agreed trump suit, you could hardly be interested in a Diamond contract) and will serve to alert partner to your interest in going on in spite of your previous sign-off.

9. Pass. Your correct procedure at this point is not at all clear, and at such times it is best to pass things around to partner and see what he has to say. This is in the nature of a forcing pass, since you made a strength showing response originally announcing at least 10 points. Partner's action should serve to clarify the picture considerably.

10. Double. Your original free raise was based on minimum values and a pass at this point might be interpreted by partner as expressing a willingness to go on. With a more unbalanced hand, we would favor a forcing pass.

11. Partner has announced that your side has the values for a game even if you have a blank. Far from being a bust, your hand has the dummy value of 12 points in support of any suit. Slam is a certainty, and in order to determine the right suit, our recommendation is a repeat of the cue bid—5 Diamonds. You will raise to 6 in whatever suit partner bids.

12. 4 Spades. Partner has shown a 6-4 distribution and it is our duty to return to his long suit, since he will be better able to stand any adverse forces there. A Heart contract might not fare well with repeated Club leads.

13. 2 Diamonds. We feel inclined to insist upon a game contract with this hand. The cue bid will enable us to proceed subsequently at a mild rate to find the best place to play this hand. Partner may have fair support for one of the majors.

14. Pass. Partner's double is very clearly for penalties. Had he wished to hear from you, he would either have doubled initially or, failing this, he would have made an Unusual Overcall in No Trump after the 2 Heart rebid. His first pass was a trap based on a strong Heart holding.

A SUMMARY OF THE
GOREN POINT COUNT METHOD
OF CONTRACT BIDDING

THE POINT COUNT TABLE

ACE = 4 POINTS

KING = 3 POINTS

QUEEN = 2 POINTS

JACK = 1 POINT

---

26 points will normally produce game. (For a minor suit game 29 points will be required.)

33 points will normally produce a small slam.

37 points will normally produce a grand slam.

Opening Bids of 1 in a Suit

In opening bids of 1 in a suit the value of a hand is determined by computing the high cards held and adding:

    3 points for a void

    2 points for each singleton

    1 point for each doubleton

13 point hands are optional openings. Bid them if convenient.

14 point hands *must* be opened.

A third hand opening may be made with 11 points, or even a little less, if a fairly good suit is held.

A fourth hand opening should be made on 13 points, even though no good rebid is available.

An Opening Demand Bid of 2 in a Suit Requires:

A good five card suit with a minimum of 25 points
A good six card suit with a minimum of 23 points
A good seven card suit with a minimum of 21 points

———

Do not make an opening pre-emptive bid on any hand containing as many as 11 points (exclusive of distribution).

Opening No Trump Bids Count High Card Values Only. No Points Are Given for Distribution.

Opening 1 No Trump—16 to 18 points
Opening 2 No Trump—22 to 24 points
Opening 3 No Trump—25 to 27 points

Responses to Opening 1 No Trump Bids:

Raise to 2 No Trump with 8 or 9 points (or 7 points with a good five card suit)

Raise to 3 No Trump with 10 to 14 points

Raise to 4 No Trump with 15 or 16 points

Raise to 6 No Trump with 17 or 18 points

Bid 3 of a suit, then 6 No Trump with 19 or 20 points

Raise to 7 No Trump with 21 points

A response of 2 Clubs shows 8 high card points and at least one four card major suit, and asks partner to show a major suit if he has one

A response of 2 Diamonds, 2 Hearts or 2 Spades shows less than 8 points, a five card suit and an unbalanced hand

A response of 4 Spades or 4 Hearts shows a long suit (six or seven cards) with less than 10 points in high cards

A response of 3 in any suit shows a hand with 10 or more points and a good suit

Responses to 2 No Trump Bids:

Raise to 3 No Trump with 4 to 8 points

Raise to 4 No Trump with 9 points

Bid 3 of a suit and then 4 No Trump with 10 points

Raise to 6 No Trump with 11 or 12 points

Bid 3 of a suit, then 6 No Trump, with 13 or 14 points

Raise to 7 No Trump with 15 points

With a five card major suit headed by an honor, and 4 points, bid that suit at the level of 3

Show any six card major suit

Bid 3 Clubs with 4 points in high cards and a four card major suit. This bid asks partner to show a major suit if he has one

Responses to 3 No Trump Bids:

Raise to 4 No Trump with 7 points

Raise to 6 No Trump with 8 or 9 points

Bid 4 Diamonds, then 6 No Trump with 10 or 11 points

Raise to 7 No Trump with 12 points

Show any five card suit if the hand contains 5 points in high cards

In Making Suit Responses Add the Distributional Points to High Card Values. Table of Valuation for Dummy Hand in Raising Partner's Suit Bid:

(A) Count high cards at face value

(B) Promote honors in partner's suit

(C) Add 1 point for each doubleton
        3 points for each singleton
        5 points for a void

(D) Deduct 1 point if your hand contains only 3 trumps
        1 point if your hand is distributed 4-3-3-3

Respond 1 No Trump with 6 to 10 points
Respond 2 No Trump with 13 to 15 points
Respond 3 No Trump with 16 to 18 points
Raise partner's suit bid to 2 with 7 to 10 points
Raise partner's suit bid to 3 with 13 to 16 points
Make a jump shift with 19 points
Show a new suit at 1 level with 6 points
Show a new suit at 2 level with 10 points
With hands counting 11 or 12 points find two bids without
forcing partner to game.

The Take-out Double

A take-out double should be based on a hand of the same
strength as an opening bid, that is, 13 points for a double
of a suit bid.

An immediate double of 1 No Trump therefore should be
based on 16 points.

When partner responds in a suit for which you have good
support, revalue your hand as dummy.

As responder to a take-out double: if you have 6 points you
have a fair hand, 9 points a good hand, and 11 points a
probable game.

As partner of the opening bidder, after a take-out double,
pass with a poor hand, redouble with a good hand, and
bid immediately with a moderate hand.

SIMON AND SCHUSTER PAPERBACKS

*For people who want to know more about science,
philosophy, the arts and history in the making*